Pathways of America:
The California Mission Trail

Written by
Lynda Hatch

Illustrated by
Don O'Connor

Good Apple
A Division of Frank Schaffer Publications, Inc.

Dedication

To the helpful, encouraging California mission historians who helped guide me through the complexity of inconsistent facts, stories, and interpretations of the mission period.

And to my friends, Jacque and John Swaney, who live near the southern missions and provided information, hospitality, and transportation; and also to my mother, Undine Sims, who traveled with me to the northern missions.

Editors: Jennifer Overend Prior, Kristin Eclov, Christine Hood
Cover Illustration: Don O'Connor
Book Design: Good Neighbor Press, Grand Junction, CO

GOOD APPLE
A Division of Frank Schaffer Publications, Inc.
23740 Hawthorne Boulevard
Torrance, CA 90505-5927

GA13055

Table of Contents

Introduction

Pathways of America: The California Mission Trail covers background information and activities on the establishment of Spain's mission system in Mexico and Alta California. The book follows El Camino Real, or "The Royal Road," connecting the missions from San Diego in the south to Sonoma in the north. Each of the 21 Catholic missions, plus one asistencia, is described and its history explained. For each mission, the story of its location, founding, successful and difficult times, secularization, and restoration is included. The book also includes maps, journal quotations, vocabulary, and a bibliography.

Quality activities for students also accompany each section. Activities teach about life at the mission through experiences in science, math, social studies, health, language arts, reading, games, music, and art. Some activities help students understand the work of the people at the mission, such as making soap, candles, weavings, roof tiles, and cattle brands. Activities are purposely designed in an open-ended manner, with few right and wrong answers, to allow students of all ages and abilities to ponder and tackle the problems. As they study life at the California missions by using the resources provided in this guide, students will become fascinated by this unique time in history. Hopefully they will choose to do additional research to answer questions that they pose themselves.

The information in this book is comprehensive and detailed and will provide the teacher with a thorough and accurate background. Teachers often don't have access to all the books that contain the amount of detail needed for their teaching, so this book can be a valuable resource. While this book attempts to cover the information accurately, as with any history, there are often differing opinions, so numerous sources were used to get the most widely accepted information. Historians from each mission were given the opportunity to review the information and were very helpful and generous with their time.

Note: The term *Indian* has been used here as it was during mission days. Today, some people prefer the term *Indian*, some prefer *Native American*, and some feel that either is fine. So as not to offend anyone, it is important to use the term that is preferred in your area.

Also note that while Spanish words and names are used in this text, accent marks have been omitted in deference to the spelling of contemporary place names. The Spanish tilde (˜), which denotes a different pronunciation of the letter *n*, has been left in place. The letter *ñ* is pronounced as if immediately followed by an *i* or *y*.

Before You Begin

As you read with students, make sure to clarify definitions for the following words, so that concepts will be easier to understand. Reading history can be difficult because of words that aren't in use today. When reading about the California missions, you will find words from English, Spanish, Italian, and a variety of Indian languages. The text in this guide is written as background information for teachers and students. Depending on individual abilities, teachers may need to guide students through the reading.

adobe	El Camino Real	pueblo (town)
agriculture	epidemic	quadrangle
alameda	faith	quarters
alcalde	fiesta	rancho
Alta California	flogging	religion
altar	Fort Ross	replica
aqueduct	Franciscan	republic
architecture	germination	reredos
artifact	governor	restoration
asistencia	gristmill	rheumatism
atole	immunity	Russians
authentic	independence	sacrament
Baja California	invalidate	saint
baptize	irrigation	scurvy
basilica	Jesuits	secularization
blacksmith	lavanderia	seminary
brand (cattle)	limestone	Spain
carreta	livestock	Spaniards
Catholic	lye (caustic soda)	Spanish
ceremony	mayordomo	swallow
chapel	Mexico	tallow
Christianity	mission chain	tanner
citrus	missionary	thatched roof
colonize	Moors/Moorish	tile
communion	neophyte	tule
companario	Order of St. Francis	uprising
convento	padre	Vatican
convert	parish	vestments
decree	poultice	viceroy
dedicate	president	vineyard
dilapidated	presidio	whitewash
earthquake	proclamation	worship

El Camino Real (The Royal Highway)

1. San Diego de Alcala
2. San Luis Rey de Francia
3. San Antonio de Pala (Asistencia)
4. San Juan Capistrano
5. San Gabriel Arcangel
6. San Fernando Rey de España
7. San Buenaventura
8. Santa Barbara
9. Santa Ines
10. La Purisima Concepcion
11. San Luis Obispo de Tolosa
12. San Miguel Arcangel
13. San Antonio de Padua
14. Nuestra Señora de la Soledad
15. San Carlos Borromeo del Rio Carmelo
16. San Juan Bautista
17. Santa Cruz
18. Santa Clara de Asis
19. San Jose
20. San Francisco de Asis
21. San Rafael Arcangel
22. San Francisco Solano

Beginning of the Missions

After the arrival of Christopher Columbus in 1492, Spain claimed much of the land in the New World. In the Catholic Church, missionary work was done by specialty groups known as orders. The Franciscan order operated missions in what are today Florida, Georgia, Texas, New Mexico, Arizona, and California.

It is surprising that it took Spain so long to explore and settle Alta California, called California today. Juan Rodriguez Cabrillo, a Portuguese explorer hired by Spain, sailed north from New Spain (Mexico) along the Pacific Coast. He arrived in California in 1542 and was impressed with the climate. Sebastian Vizcaino sailed up the coast in 1602 and was so enthusiastic that he urged Spain to colonize California, but it wasn't done until years later. Beginning in 1697, they started establishing Jesuit missions in Baja California, the Mexican peninsula south of present-day California, but hadn't explored lands to the north. Deserts and mountains blocked the land route north, and it was difficult sailing up the western coast of Baja California due to strong headwinds. So little was known about California that it was mapped as an island as late as the mid-18th century.

In 1767, King Carlos III of Spain expelled the Jesuits in Baja California because he thought that they were hiding pearls and gold due to the royal treasury. Don Gaspar de Portola was the soldier sent to remove the Jesuits. De Portola was given the title of Governor of the Californias. The priest who took over the Jesuit chain of 14 missions was a Franciscan missionary named Junipero Serra.

Jose de Galvez, the king's inspector-general, wanted to send men to extend the Spanish frontier to Alta California in the north. He convinced the king that it was a race against time to have these lands come under the control of Spain.

Spanish attitudes toward settling Alta California changed when news got back to Spain that in around 1745, the Russians had crossed the Bering Strait and started a settlement in Kodiak, Alaska. The Spanish became concerned as the Russians built fur trading forts and settlements down the coast, north of what is today San Francisco. Russians, English, and explorers from other countries might try to take over lands that Cabrillo and Vizcaino had already claimed for Spain.

In 1768, Carlos III authorized the Mexican viceroy to occupy San Diego and Monterey, starting the exploration and settlement of Alta California. The Catholic Church was an important influence in Spain, so it became part of the Spanish colonial plan. Spain sent groups of soldiers with padres to colonize new lands. The Spanish partnership of the sword and the cross had been very successful, especially in South America. (In addition to guard soldiers at each mission, military presidios were established at Monterey, San Francisco, San Diego, and Santa Barbara to guard against European powers, pirates, and hostile Indians.) The government was interested in riches and trade, while the padres were looking for souls to save.

This clergy/military partnership was a cost-effective arrangement for the government. Missions were inexpensive to start because the padres received no pay and had few needs, and the missions were soon self-supporting. The presence of the missions would help keep the land under control of Spain. Each mission would be the beginning of a civilian town and would be located at regular intervals throughout Alta California.

When missions were built near harbors, towns could develop that would be good for trade, and the traders wouldn't try to claim the land for themselves. The missions were important to the government's plan for building an empire. Few Spaniards were willing to settle these new, remote lands. With few people available to follow the padres, it was hoped that colonies would be established, using the local Indians. They hoped to educate Indians enough to change them into "civilized Spaniards," or colonists of their own land. The Indians would be able to run a pueblo, subject to civil law, and under the spiritual guidance of parish clergy.

The padres were motivated by more than merely helping Spain colonize new lands. The Franciscans, who were given the responsibility of founding the Alta California missions, were followers of St. Francis of Assisi. They were religious men who hoped to convert the Indians to Christianity in order to save their souls. Padres had a tremendous influence on the early days of California—from 1769, when Padre Serra left Mexico for San Diego, until the end around 1833. The missions reached the height of their power between 1800 and 1812.

Jesuit Missions of
Baja California and New Spain

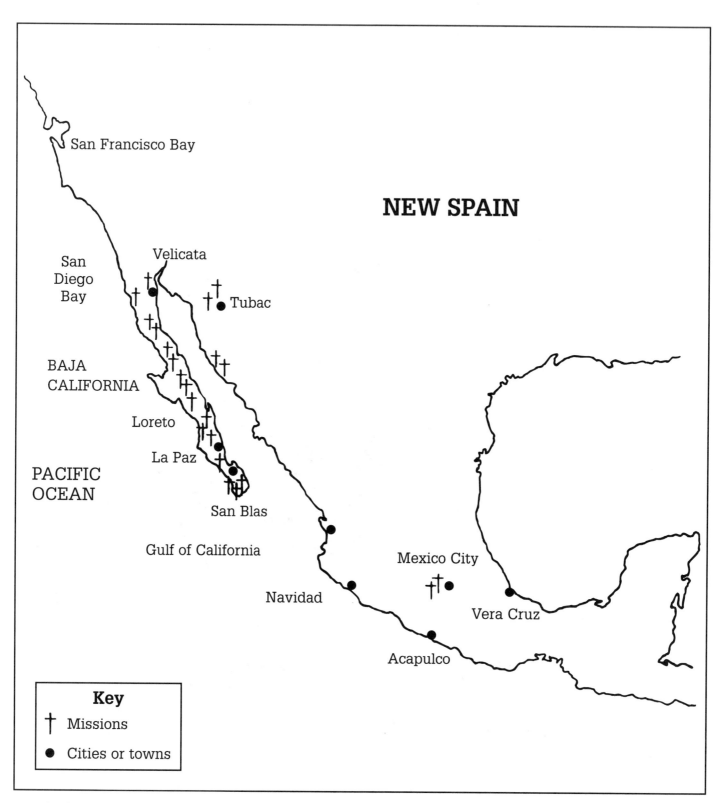

NEW SPAIN

San Francisco Bay

San
Diego
Bay

Velicata

Tubac

BAJA
CALIFORNIA

Loreto

La Paz

PACIFIC
OCEAN

San Blas

Gulf of California

Mexico City

Navidad

Vera Cruz

Acapulco

Key
† Missions
● Cities or towns

Mission Postage Stamp

On August 22, 1985, a commemorative postage stamp was issued, honoring Padre Junipero Serra. It was a 44-cent airmail stamp. The stamp shows a mission, map, and portrait of Serra.

Almost all subjects chosen to appear on U.S. stamps are suggested by the public. The U.S. Postal Service receives and responds to hundreds of suggestions every week, but only a few are selected. By law, the Postmaster General has the final authority to decide on stamp subjects, but also relies on the recommendations of the Citizens' Stamp Advisory Committee. This committee is made up of historians, artists, business people, stamp collectors, and others interested in American history and culture. The committee has guidelines for selecting new stamps. Once a subject is chosen, a professional artist designs the stamp. The committee reviews preliminary artwork and may ask for changes before a final version goes to the Postmaster General.

A *commemorative* stamp is one that honors an anniversary, important person, or special event. They are usually only sold for a certain length of time.

Commemorative stamps are the opposite of *definitive* stamps. These are regular issues of stamps, usually sold over long periods of time.

Activity

Imagine that the U.S. Postal Service has asked you to design a commemorative postage stamp, honoring the California missions.

1. Choose an aspect of the California missions for your commemorative stamp, such as a person, building, mission lifestyle, or event.

2. Draw the picture on 8½" x 11" (21.5 cm x 28 cm) white paper, using very simple lines. Your stamp will be drawn large, but since real stamps are small, it should not have extensive details.

3. Color your stamp with crayons, colored pencils, markers, or paints.

4. Using a single-hole punch, evenly punch around the outside of your paper, making half-circle punches. (These holes will look like stamp perforations. Perforations are lines of small holes between two rows of stamps that make the stamps easy to tear apart.)

5. Glue your stamp to a piece of colored construction paper that goes well with the colors on your stamp. Display your mission stamp.

Land and Sea Journeys to Alta California

Padre Junipero Serra was the Spanish missionary given the task of establishing missions in Alta California. The viceroy, the king's representative in Mexico, told Serra, "You will be head of a new mission system—at each there will be a church, workshops, small houses, crops, and classes in Spanish and religion." Along with the missions, the Spaniards would build presidios (forts) for guard soldiers. Pueblos (towns) would be built where colonies of families from Mexico would settle. Serra had been born in a tiny village on the island of Majorca, Spain. He had done an excellent job working with the Indians in Mexican missions, so his name was suggested to King Carlos III of Spain as the man who should do the same with the Indians of Alta California. The king gave the orders to "occupy and fortify San Diego and Monterey for God and the king of Spain."

Three expeditions were sent by sea and two by land in 1769; all were to meet together to start the first new mission near San Diego Bay. The ships carried supplies that would be needed in Alta California, such as corn, wheat, peas, wine, and farming tools. Materials were also sent for church services, such as altars, bells, candles, and priests' robes. One ship, the *San Jose*, sank with its crew and supplies. The *San Antonio* and the *San Carlos* were blown off course. Due to the long trip, sailors from both ships got scurvy, and many of the crew died and were buried at sea. (Scurvy is a disease caused by the lack of vitamin C. Teeth loosen, gums soften, and there is bleeding under the skin.)

It took the first land expedition two months to travel the difficult 350 miles from El Rosario to San Diego Bay. In his diary, Padre Juan Crespi described the land as "sterile, arid, lacking grass and water, and abounding in stones and thorns." Soldiers and Indian converts were also

part of the group. Of the 50 Indians, five died and about 30 deserted. The pack mules carried food, tools, and seeds. The men tried to travel with too many other animals and had difficulty finding food and water, which slowed the trip.

The second land expedition left Baja California with Padre Serra and Captain Gaspar de Portola, the military governor, as leaders. They visited other Mexican missions along the way and gathered supplies from them. Portola wrote, "I was obliged to seize everything I saw as I passed through those poor missions, leaving them, to my keen regret, scantily provided for." Even so, the men ran out of food. On this trip, Serra's leg became infected from an untreated insect bite that had bothered him for 30 years. He was in such pain that Portola almost had the group return to Mexico. Serra convinced a muleteer to treat his wound with a poultice used for his mules! The leg improved and they were able to continue, but the injury continued to bother him for the rest of his life.

On July 1, 1769, the land and sea groups were reunited, but they were in very poor condition. Of the 219 people who started the journey, almost half had died. Their food was almost gone, and some of the men wanted to return to Mexico. The padres and Portola didn't give up because they knew how important the missions and presidios were to Spain and the Catholic Church. The *San Antonio*, with a small crew of just eight men (of the original 28), was sent back to Baja California to get fresh supplies and new crews for the two ships. Only two men were alive when it arrived in San Blas.

Champurrado Chocolate Drink

When the first land expedition was on its difficult journey to San Diego, they ran out of their jerked beef supply. They could only eat one tortilla and one cup of chocolate a day. Drinking chocolate was a standard food among the Spanish at the missions in the early days. It was preferred over coffee because of its nutrients and because it was easy to get. They liked it thicker than we drink it today.

Activity

There are many recipes for Spanish chocolate drinks, but here is one you may wish to make.

Ingredients

2 tablespoons (30 mL) grated chocolate

2 tablespoons (30 mL) sugar

1 cup (250 mL) very hot water

5 cups (1.25 L) milk, scalded

2 tablespoons (30 mL) cornstarch

2 eggs, well beaten

2 teaspoons (10 mL) vanilla

Dash cinnamon or nutmeg

Directions

In a double boiler, combine the cocoa and sugar. Slowly add the hot water, stirring until the mixture forms a smooth paste. Cook the mixture for five minutes. Add the scalded milk a little at a time over low heat. Add the cornstarch, which has been blended with some of the hot liquid. When it is very hot and just before serving, add the beaten eggs, vanilla, and cinnamon or nutmeg. Whip the mixture until it is frothy.

Note: In the morning, the padres usually ate chocolate and toast or biscuits. About 11:00 in the morning, they had glasses of brandy with pieces of cake and cheese. The noon dinner might consist of vermicelli; rice or bread soup; beef or mutton stew; ham with beans, lentils, or Spanish peas; and greens. Dessert was usually fresh or dried fruit, sweetmeats, and cheese. There was also wine. Supper was served between 7:00 and 8:00 in the evening. They might have had roast pigeon or other fowl and chocolate. Other dishes were prepared when there were guests.

San Diego de Alcala Mission

City: San Diego, Mission Valley
Founded: July 16, 1769
Order of founding: 1st
Founder: Padre Junipero Serra

San Diego de Alcala was the first mission founded in Alta (Northern) California, so it was known as the "Mother of the Missions." It was one of the most difficult to begin and maintain.

Serra and Portola had traveled to Alta California to start a chain of Catholic Franciscan missions. After resting at San Diego Bay, Portola and a small group of men continued north to try to find Monterey Bay. After Portola left, Serra had the men who were well enough build a chapel and a hospital out of poles and tules. Serra blessed these first mission buildings at San Diego. The ceremony that was used at the founding of this mission became the pattern for the founding of the other missions. A large wooden cross was raised, mass was said, the local Indians were called by bells hung from trees and were given trinkets to win their confidence.

Six months later, Portola returned from Monterey. He found the people at San Diego in terrible condition, and more had died. The few buildings were in poor shape, and the supply ship, *San Antonio*, had not yet returned after seven months. Portola ordered everyone to return to Mexico. Serra pleaded with him to wait nine more days for the ship to arrive, until March 19, St. Joseph's Day. He felt that if they gave up, the Indians would not learn about Christianity. Portola agreed to wait, but was sure the ship would not arrive. At 3:00 in the afternoon on the ninth day, sails were sighted, so Portola agreed to wait a while longer. The supply ship arrived in the bay four days later.

In 1774, the mission at San Diego was moved six miles upriver. The new site was closer to water, to the Indian villages, and to fields for farming. The move was also done to keep the Indians away from the military men at the presidio. A presidio was an armed fort of Spanish soldiers who were sent to keep the peace and protect the Spanish from Indians. Since many of the Spanish guards were tough convicts, the padres were concerned for the Indians' safety. The new mission buildings were built of logs and thatched roofs. The mission grew slowly.

The Indians were curious about the Spaniards, but they didn't trust them. Even though they were fascinated by woven fabric, gifts of cloth would not make them stay either. To get fabric, the Indians supposedly removed bed sheets from sick soldiers and tried to cut the sails from the supply ship, the *San Carlos*. They also wouldn't accept gifts of food, believing it was the cause of the Spaniards' sickness. Serra prayed that the Indians would come to be baptized. However, the few Indians who did visit the mission were frightened and wouldn't stay.

One Indian boy, however, came to visit the padres. Serra asked the child to convince a father to have his baby baptized. Serra was happy when the father agreed. But just before the baptism, another Indian snatched the baby away and ran off to the village. Serra was so upset that for a long time his eyes filled with tears when he told the story.

In the early years of the mission, there was frequent violence between the Spanish and Indians. Although some Indians were being baptized, things were not as peaceful as they seemed. The Indians were angered by the way Spanish soldiers treated Indian women, by the punishments for breaking Spanish rules, and by the Spaniards moving onto their lands.

In 1775, between 600 and 1,000 Indians surrounded the mission at night, set it on fire, and stole what they could carry. Padre Luis Jayme was killed in this attack when he tried to calm the Indians. The Indians felt that he was trying to take people away from their tribes. The rest of the people escaped to the presidio for protection. The raid delayed the founding of other missions until more soldiers could arrive. However, the failed raid also discouraged Indians from trying to drive out the Spaniards.

In 1776, Serra began the construction of a new church and mission buildings. To make the building more fire-resistant, adobe covered the walls and the roof was made of tiles. The buildings were arranged in a quadrangle around a patio. The second church was damaged by an earthquake in 1803. Between 1808 and 1813, the mission was restored and enlarged. Two massive buttresses were built to help the new sanctuary survive future earthquakes.

At secularization in 1834, Mexican officials took over lands that were supposed to go to the Indians. The Indians were left with nothing and had to go back to living as they had before mission days. On June 8, 1846, the Mexican governor, Pio Pico, gave away the mission and many acres of land to Santiago Arguello as a reward for his service to the government.

In 1847, when the U.S. gained control of California, an army cavalry troop moved into the mission. The church was remodeled into a two-story barrack. On and off until 1862, soldiers lived upstairs and the horse stalls were on the bottom level. Many church objects were destroyed. The army tore down buildings that it didn't feel were safe and made temporary repairs to others. Doors and windows were cut through the adobe walls, causing the building to erode into ruins even faster. In 1862, President Abraham Lincoln returned 22 acres of mission property to the Catholic Church—but by then, the mission was in ruins.

In the 1880s, an Indian school was started in some of the rooms of the old mission. Father Anthony ran the school and spent over 20 years trying to restore the mission. Restoration slowed when he died in 1907, but a major effort to rebuild the mission started again in 1931. It was restored as closely as possible to the 1813 church. Today, the church is an active Catholic parish.

San Diego de Alcala Mission

Making Glass "Bells"

Activity

Learn how high and low sounds can be made by glasses of the same size filled with different levels of water.

1. Fill glasses (or jars) with different amounts of water.

2. With a metal spoon, gently tap the glasses and listen to the sounds that are created.

3. Adjust the amount of water to play simple songs. Try songs with a range of about five notes, such as "Mary Had a Little Lamb" or "Sweetly Sings the Donkey."

Note: All sounds are made by vibrations. Things that vibrate quickly make high sounds, and those that vibrate slowly make low sounds. Pitch is the highness or lowness of sound. When the glass is tapped, the glass vibrates and makes sound. The pitch can be changed by adding different amounts of water. The glass with the least amount of water will have the lowest pitch, since only a small part of the glass vibrates. The glass with the most water will have the highest pitch, since more of the glass vibrates. This can also be done with pop bottles. Instead of tapping on the bottles, blow across the top to produce sound. The results will be the opposite as when the bottles were tapped. It is the air in the bottles that vibrates, so that the bottle with the least air (most water) will have the highest pitch, and the one with the most air (least water) will have the lowest pitch.

San Diego de Alcala is known for its beautiful bell tower (or wall) called a campanario. This three-tiered campanario is 46 feet (14 meters) tall and rises above the mission garden. It is a single tower, not attached to the church. Of the five bells, two are from the original mission church. One bell has a crown top, showing that it was supplied by the Spanish king, and is therefore called a "royal" bell. The largest bell weighs 1,200 pounds. It was cast in San Diego in 1894 from five bells sent to the mission by the viceroy in 1796.

At all the missions, the ringing of the bells controlled the daily lives of the Indians and Spaniards. The bells called people to work, meals, and church. Bells also announced daily happenings, the arrival of visitors, special events, festivals, weddings, and baptisms.

It took much practice to ring the heavy bells without getting hit and to create the proper sounds. The Indians considered it an honor to ring them. Some Indians even continued to ring the bells in abandoned mission churches long after the missions were active.

Campanario (Bell Tower)

San Luis Rey de Francia Mission

City: San Luis Rey, near Oceanside
Founded: June 13, 1798
Order of founding: 18th
Founder: Padre Fermin de Lasuen

Although San Luis Rey de Francia was one of the last missions to be founded, it was one of the most successful. It was built on a low hill in an inland valley. Padre de Lasuen chose this site because of the great number of Indians living in the area. Many were eager to become part of the mission. San Luis Rey became known as the "King of the Missions," because it served the largest Indian population of any mission (between 2,000 and 3,000 Indians). It was the largest of the California missions, covering six acres. Up until the mid-1800s, the mission church was the largest structure in California.

The mission grew rapidly under the energetic leadership of Padre Antonio Peyri. He was 29 years old when the mission was founded, and he stayed as its administrator for 34 years! He was a popular and loving padre who was respected by the Indians. Pablo Tac wrote about his life as an Indian at the mission. He said of Peyri, "If anyone wants anything, he will ask the missionary, who will immediately give him whatever he asks, because he is the father of all."

The church was built in a "cross" shape. It was one of the larger mission churches and could hold a thousand worshippers. A large wooden dome rose above the sanctuary, the only ceiling of its kind among the California missions. The church was so spectacular that a French visitor in 1828 called it a "palace."

The mission had an elaborate water system for laundry, bathing, drinking, and irrigation. Water was channeled into "sunken gardens" where

many fruits and vegetables were grown. The mission was also known for its grapes, oranges, and olives. The first pepper tree in California was planted in the mission's Friary Garden. It provided the padres with peppercorns, which they ground for seasoning.

From the beginning, the Luiseño Indians were generally accepting of life at the mission. Since most of the Indians preferred their own houses, there was no adobe village at the mission. Instead, they lived in their villages. Because of the detailed account written by Pablo Tac, more is known about the daily life at San Luis Rey than at any other mission. He said that in his home each morning, his family had a breakfast consisting of a hot drink, meat, and tortillas. His father went hunting with a bow and arrow or gathered wood. His mother stayed home to cook and do other chores. Younger children went to school at the mission, while older children and adults worked at businesses, farms, or ranches. At noon, everyone went home for lunch; then they went back to their work until the middle of the afternoon. There was another meal in the evening, and then everyone went to bed.

The early 1830s were the most prosperous years for the mission. But then, the Mexican government, which had broken away from Spain's rule, took over the management of California missions. With the growing number of settlers from Mexico, there was increasing demand to take the mission lands away from the Indians. Padre Peyri tried to get along with the Mexican officials, but he became upset with the government's opposition to the mission system and by the efforts to convince the Indians to give up their lands to settlers in exchange for food or whiskey. The Indians had no way to earn a living and no one was left to tend the mission fields. Peyri wanted to leave before the mission was completely destroyed. He secretly asked to quit his job.

In 1832, Peyri left in the middle of the night, hoping to avoid painful farewells to his Indian friends at San Luis Rey. When he was missed the next morning, they guessed what he had done, and 500 Indians rushed 30 miles to the beach at San Diego. They caught up with him as he was about to sail for Spain and pleaded with him to return. He knew he had to go, but with tears flowing down his cheeks, he gave them a farewell blessing from the deck of the ship as it sailed out of the harbor. Many of the Indians swam toward the ship to plead with their beloved padre not to leave them. It is said that they prayed for his safe return for many years. After secularization, the mission quickly decayed and the Indians returned to the hills.

The abandoned San Luis Rey mission was used as a U.S. military outpost during and after the Mexican War. Soldiers sometimes broke in and took church furnishings. The mission turned to ruins. California became part of the United States in 1850 as the 31st state. In 1865, President Abraham Lincoln signed a decree returning the mission to the Catholic Church.

The mission remained abandoned and was not used for religious purposes until 1893. Under the leadership of Padre Joseph Jeremiah O'Keefe, Franciscan padres started a seminary at the mission where young men studied to be priests. Reconstruction started with O'Keefe and has continued to the present. Today the mission is also a parish church and conference center.

Mission Construction

Not only was Padre Antonio Peyri a good priest, he also had a talent for architecture. Because Peyri was the administrator at the mission for 34 years, building was probably more coordinated than at any other mission. Building construction was almost continually in progress. His efforts resulted in one of the best-designed mission churches. The mission is beautiful, with its brilliant white exterior and its blue-capped bell tower.

Although each mission looked different, there were many similarities between them. Missions were usually built around a courtyard (or patio) in the shape of a quadrangle (square), with the church in one corner. Workshops, storerooms, dining and cooking facilities, and guest and living quarters were placed around the square. Only one or two doors led out of the quadrangle. They were locked at night for protection.

The padres were not trained engineers or architects. They read books about building and design and included building features that they remembered from Mexico or Spain. The padres drew their plans on paper to guide the workmen. Usually they had just a few trained artisans or experienced workmen.

Because adobe bricks were so heavy, the walls had to be 4–5 feet (1.25–1.5 meters) thick in order to hold their weight and the weight of the tile roofs. The wide eaves and roofed corridors helped protect the adobe walls from the rain so they wouldn't erode. Bricks were made by stomping adobe clay. Water and straw were then mixed with the clay and placed into wooden molds. Bricks were 23" (5.75 cm) long, 11" (28 cm) wide, and 2–5" (5–12.75 cm) thick. They were laid in the sun to dry. The bricks were stacked on top of each other and held together with mud. The walls were finished with plaster made of a water, lime, and sand mixture. Lime was found in seashells and limestone rock. In the early years, the roofs were thatched with straw, but later they were made with red tiles.

Activity

Construct a mission layout. You have many choices:

1. Work together or with others.

2. Copy the layout of a specific mission or build a layout of a general mission plan.

3. Building blocks (glued together with white glue) can be made from a variety of materials, such as

   a. sugar cubes.

   b. miniature bricks made from three parts powdered terra cotta clay to one part sand, and enough water to make a workable substance. A little straw can be added to make them look more authentic. Mold them in small matchboxes.

   c. carved Styrofoam blocks—cut very gently with a sharp knife.

   d. bricks made from other types of clay, adding coloring if needed.

4. Roofs can be made from materials that look like tiles, such as corrugated cardboard or lasagna noodles painted a reddish tile color.

5. Label the buildings so others can learn the layout of your mission.

San Antonio de Pala Asistencia Mission

City: Pala
Founded: June 13, 1816
Order of founding: Asistencia
Founder: Padre Antonio Peyri

The missions served a wide area, and sometimes "ranchos" and additional chapels were built to help serve the large mission. Pala was one of these "asistencias," or branch chapels, of the San Luis Rey mission.

The Pala Indians were named Luiseños by the missionaries. Their village was about 20 miles inland from the mission. The soil was good, and farmers from San Luis Rey began growing corn in Pala before the mission was established. The mission was very successful. The founder, Padre Peyri, said, "San Luis Rey has a station called San Antonio de Pala, with a church, dwellings, and granaries, and with a few fields where wheat, corn, beans, garbanzos, and other leguminous plants are grown. There is also a vineyard and an orchard of various fruits and olives."

The chapel is the original, built in 1816. Two years after it was founded, the chapel was enlarged, and other buildings were added. The chapel has original Indian paintings on the walls. The Indian culture is blended with religious images of the Catholic Church. For example, the chapel contains an Indian statue called "Our lady–Mulu' wetam," in the Cupeño language, meaning "Our lady of the first people."

Pala's bell tower is unusual, as it is completely detached from the church building. On top of the bell tower, next to the cross, is a cactus. There are two legends as to how the cactus was planted.

1) Padre Peyri planted it to show that mission construction was completed.

2) As soon as Peyri placed the cross on the top, a bird landed on the arms of the cross. The bird sang joyously. When it opened its mouth to praise God, a cactus seed dropped on the soft adobe and from it sprang a mature cactus.

After secularization in 1835, the mission rancho deteriorated. New settlers stripped the buildings of roof tiles and timbers. Because the buildings were made of adobe (clay), the exposed areas soon washed away in the rain. The remote location of Pala, however, protected it from being totally destroyed. The chapel and west wing of the building remained. The rest of the buildings were reconstructed by 1959. In 1903, the Cupeño Indians were moved to Pala and it is still their home.

Today, the mission is again administered by Franciscan friars. The mission school was reestablished in 1958 and is the only one of the original California mission schools still serving the Indians whom it first served. The work started by the Franciscan padres in 1816 continues at Pala today.

California Indian Games

Activity

Try this California Indian game:

Nut-Dice Game

This was mostly a woman's game, but it can be played by everyone today.

Materials

- empty walnut shells, used like dice
- 200 sticks or tiny bones, used as score counters
- basket for storing the materials

Directions

Shake the walnut shells in your hands and toss them into the basket. Take a stick or bone for every point you make.

- Three shells up and three shells down gives the player two points.
- All shells tossed on one side gives the player three points.
- No other combination scores points.
- The game is over when the sticks or bones are used up.

The Indians, including those at Pala, shared their ways of life with the Spanish and other groups who came to California. Some Indian games played during mission days can still can be enjoyed today.

Note: Some activities listed as "games" in books are not considered mere fun by today's Native Americans. For example, while the game of Peon is often played by children, it was originally a spiritual pastime for medicine men. Today it is played separately by men and women. It is not considered a game, but rather part of a much larger spiritual experience. Pairs of bones, some tied with sinew bands and some left unmarked, are hidden in the hands of some players. Other players try to guess which bones are marked with sinew and which are not. Be sensitive about activities that are not true games and should not be played without a complete understanding of their purpose.

San Juan Capistrano Mission

City: San Juan Capistrano
Founded: October 30, 1775, and again on November 1, 1776
Order: 7th
Founder: Padre de Lasuen, and then by Padre Serra

San Juan Capistrano was founded twice. Padre de Lasuen was sent by Padre Serra to start this new mission. De Lasuen hung bells from a tree, put out a wooden cross, and dedicated the site on October 30, 1775. A crowd of Indians watched the ceremony and helped haul timber for the construction of a temporary chapel. A few soldiers, Indians, and Padre de Lasuen had only worked eight days when they suddenly stopped. A horseman arrived, announcing an Indian attack on the San Diego mission. The Spanish feared that they might be attacked, too. The founding of the mission would have to wait. They buried the heavy church bells and hurried to San Diego, where the presidio soldiers could protect them.

A year later, when they felt it was safe, the San Juan Capistrano Mission was founded again, this time by Padre Serra on November 1, 1776. By the summer of 1778, a small adobe chapel had been built and is still in use today. It is considered the oldest church in California. It is called "Father Serra's Church," because it is thought to be the only remaining church where Serra is known to have celebrated mass.

By 1795, the mission had grown so large that the chapel became too small. Padre Vicente Fuster planned a huge stone church that would be the most impressive in the whole mission chain. An expert stone mason, Isidro Aguilar, was brought from Mexico to supervise the construction of the church. For nine years, the priests and Indians worked hard on the construction, carrying, carting, and cementing rocks for the 7-foot (2.25-meter) thick walls. The church was built in the shape of a cross, with seven ceiling domes and a 120-foot (36.5-meter) bell tower that could be seen for ten miles. The design and construction of this cathedral-like church was so beautiful and sophisticated that San Juan Capistrano became known as "The Jewel of the Missions."

This elaborate church stood for just six years. An earthquake struck at the end of an early morning church service on December 8, 1812. Just as the bells began to ring for the next mass, there was a deep rumble and the bells rang wildly in a jangled discord. Walls swayed and broke, dumping the concrete ceiling on the helpless worshipers. The only people saved were those who were able to follow the frantic directions of the padres and escape to the sanctuary. Forty bodies were dug out of the rubble. The two boys who had been ringing the bells in the tower were killed, but the mass had been for adults only, so no other children died. The mission recovered from the tragedy. It was unthinkable to rebuild such a large church, so the padres moved back into the small Father Serra's Church.

The mission was one of the most successful. It was located in a beautiful valley with a mild climate, rich soil for crops, and generous water supply. Being close to the ocean, the mission became a trade center for ships. The mission had large herds of sheep, horses, and cattle. Twenty-thousand head of cattle and sheep roamed over the mission's eight ranchos.

Every part of the cattle was used. In brick pits, the fat and bones were boiled down into tallow for soap, candles, grease, and ointments. Cattle hides were soaked in tannic acid, stretched, and dried in the sun. The Indians made hides into leather goods such as saddles and sandals. The processing of hides was a large industry and used in trade called "leather dollars." Writer, Richard Henry Dana described how hides were thrown down cliffs to the beach and taken to trading ships: "Down this height we pitched the hides, throwing them as far out into the air as we could; and as they were all large, stiff, and doubled like the cover of a book, the wind took them, and swayed them about, plunging and rising in the air, like a kite when it has broken its string."

After the bell tower was destroyed in the earthquake, the bells were hung in the existing campanario. The bells are still rung in an unusual manner, by pulling ropes tied to each clapper, instead of swinging the supports above the bells. All work, church services, meals, and recreation started and ended at a signal from the bells. Tales were told of the bells ringing by themselves at tragic or romantic moments. Padre John O'Sullivan, who spent 23 years restoring the mission, wrote about one story: "There lived with her parents near the mission an Indian maid named Matilda, who was very gentle and devout, and who loved to care for the sanctuary and to keep fresh flowers on the altars. She took sick, however, and died just at the break of day. Immediately, in order to announce her departure, the four bells all began of their own accord, or rather, by the hands of angels, to ring together. . . ."

After the 1833 secularization, the mission began to decline. The Indians were supposedly "freed," but the government was more interested in the mission lands than the care of the Indians. Padre O'Sullivan described what happened to the Indians whose lands were confiscated by government officials: ". . . the Indians, deprived of their lands and the fruit of their labor—cattle, horses, implements, vineyards, gardens and all—became either attached as servants to ranchers to work for mere rations or eke out a miserable existence in their own huts until smallpox and other diseases wiped them out."

On December 4, 1845, the Mexican governor, Pio Pico, auctioned the mission buildings, furniture, three plots of land, the garden, the orchard, and the vineyard to Juan Forster, his brother-in-law and partner, for $710.00. It was paid to Pico in cash, hides, and tallow. When the United States acquired California, the sale was declared illegal. On March 18, 1865, President Abraham Lincoln signed a decree returning the mission buildings and land back to the church. It was too late to help the Indians, however, because very few Juanenos had survived.

Over time, the buildings were neglected and deteriorated rapidly after the tile and timber was taken by settlers. In an attempted restoration of the church in the 1860s,

gunpowder was used to destroy piles of stone, which only further damaged the church. In 1895, the Landmarks Club raised restoration money to replace the roofs and put supports on the few mission walls left standing. This probably saved the mission from complete ruin.

A major restoration was begun when Father John O'Sullivan arrived. He had been ill with tuberculosis, a disease that normally killed people in those days. He came to California hoping that the climate would be good for his lungs. He loved the mission and asked to be put in charge of the ruins. At first, he lived in a tent on the patio because the buildings were infested by insects. He began to restore the mission himself and then hired Mexican workers to build walls and make paints in the old ways of mission days. As his work continued over 23 years, he recovered from his illness. He worked hard to restore Father Serra's Church. Fortunately, the walls had stayed intact because the roof had been kept in repair. It had been leased for several years as a storehouse for olives, wood, and barley.

In 1918, O'Sullivan was given permission to make the mission into an active church again. The most ambitious restoration project was a ten-year stabilization and preservation project started after the 1987 Whittier earthquake.

Swallows

San Juan Capistrano is probably best known for the stories, songs, and poems about the swallows that return to their nests at the mission every spring. It is fitting that the founder of the Franciscans, St. Francis of Assisi, once called all birds his brothers. The swallows migrate 2,000 miles from Central America each St. Joseph's Day, March 19th. Some of the birds arrive at the mission early and some late, if delayed by winter storms, but most do arrive around the 19th. The first swallows to arrive are usually scouts that nested at the mission the year before. The swallows begin repairing old nests and building new ones under the eaves of the mission buildings. The gourd-like nests are made from mud gathered from streams and ponds. It is mixed with saliva that helps the mud harden without cracking. (They fly south for the winter around October 23rd, St. John's Day.)

These birds are cliff swallows (*Petrochelidon pyrrhonota*), also called las golondrinas in Spanish. They are not the same as their fork-tailed cousins, the barn swallows. Cliff swallows are small, 5½" (14–cm) brown birds with blue-black caps, backs, wings, and tails. They have a rusty red color on their rumps and throats and cream-white foreheads. They are busy birds, constantly swooping and diving for airborne insects. Because they eat many insects, they are a benefit to farmers. The food supply of swallows is dwindling because of fewer open fields, especially near creekbeds. Swallows fascinate mission visitors with their swift and graceful aerial maneuvers. However, it is more often pigeons that visitors feed in the mission courtyard! Cliff swallows are also common at the San Carlos Borromeo de Carmelo mission.

Mission San Juan Capistrano celebrates St. Joseph's Day, when the swallows return to the mission. Crowds gather to greet the swallows. The famous song, "When the Swallows Come Back to Capistrano" is performed. Local Native Americans perform dances and bake traditional bread. Living history characters and dancers represent mission days in colorful costumes.

Activity

Mission San Juan Capistrano became famous because of its swallows. Using factual information about cliff swallows, write a story, poem, or song. Your creation should contain swallow facts, yet should be written in a creative, original, and artistic manner.

San Gabriel Arcangel Mission

City: San Gabriel, near Los Angeles
Founded: September 8, 1771
Order of founding: 4th
Founder: Padre Junipero Serra

In the summer of 1771, Padre Serra chose the site for the San Gabriel Arcangel mission. He sent Padres Pedro Cambon and Angel Somera and guard soldiers to start the mission. It was founded near Rio do los Temblores (River of Earthquakes), because four earthquakes shook the area the day it was named by the Spanish. When the padres and soldiers arrived at the river, trying to decide on an exact location for the mission, they were surrounded by a large group of yelling Indians. Fearing an attack, they opened a large banner showing the Indians a painting of Mary, the mother of Jesus. At the sight of the beautiful painting, the Indians threw down their bows and arrows and became quiet. The Spaniards felt that the influence of the painting on the Indians was a miracle. This 300-year-old painting, *Our Lady of Sorrows*, can still be seen at the mission.

Soon after the founding of the mission, an unfortunate incident occurred that destroyed the Gabrielino Indians' confidence in the mission. The soldiers were supposed to keep order, but they had trouble getting along with the Indians. One of the soldiers mistreated the wife of an Indian chief. The Indians tried to kill the soldier, but in the skirmish the chief was killed. The chief's head was cut off and impaled on a pole to warn against further attacks. The Indians didn't trust the soldiers or padres. Padres Cambon and Somera became ill and were replaced by Padres Paterna and Antonio Cruzado. They were gentle and understanding, and gradually regained the confidence of the Indians.

In 1772, Padres de Lasuen and Palou visited San Gabriel. Only a few crude buildings remained, and spring floods had ruined the crops. They recommended moving the mission. In 1775, it was moved about five miles to a higher and drier site.

Padre Sanchez replaced Paterna in 1776. Padres Cruzado and Sanchez worked together for nearly 30 years and made San Gabriel an agricultural success. Today, because the mission is surrounded by urban Los Angeles it is hard to imagine the 90 acres of agricultural fields of mission days. San Gabriel was located in a fertile valley with timber, pastures, and plenty of water for irrigation. The climate was gentle. It became known as the "Mother of California Agriculture" because of its prosperity in producing more crops than all other missions. The padres grew abundant crops of corn, beans, peas, lentils, barley, and garbanzos. They planted the first Valencia orange grove at this mission with seedlings from Spain. There were also large orchards of olives, lemons, pears, peaches, apples, and figs. The mission also became famous for its fine wines. It had the oldest and at one time largest winery in California. There were also large herds of cattle branded with the letter *T*. The *T* stood for *temblores* (earthquakes). This was an appropriate name, since there were several earthquakes in the area during the mission's early years.

The new church was started in 1779 and finished in 1805. This fortress-like building was built of stone, concrete, and brick. San Gabriel was built in a unique Moorish design, inspired by the cathedral at Cordova, Spain, where Padre Cruzado had studied. The design was also unusual in that the facade is a side wall with the main entrance on the side. The mission contains remarkable Indian paintings done on canvas, probably from ship sails. The colors are still bright after all these years. A 10-foot (3-meter) wall of cacti served as a hedge around much of the property. Part of the cactus hedge and orchards can still be seen around the town of San Gabriel.

For the next 20 years, Padre Jose Zalvidea carried on the mission's work. The 1812 earthquake greatly damaged the monastery and toppled the church tower. In 1828, the church was completely restored. Zalvidea had an Indian hospital built. He was a very hard worker with great physical strength and deep religious conviction; he was a born leader.

In 1781, settlers took up homestead land about nine miles northwest of San Gabriel. The mission became the spiritual and cultural center for this new, growing pueblo of Los Angeles.

The mission even became a shipyard! It is thought that the 99-ton schooner *Guadalupe* was built at San Gabriel. It was then disassembled and hauled to San Pedro on carretas and launched. In 1831, the ship was sailed to Mazatlan and San Blas, Mexico, and loaded with mission goods.

The mission lands were secularized in 1834. The Mexican governor, Pio Pico, somehow acquired the mission lands. Just before his death, he gave the mission to two Americans in payment of a debt. This deal was later declared illegal. Indians remained on the land and the church was cared for by successive Franciscan padres. When President Buchanan restored the property to the Catholic Church in 1859, the church itself was in good shape, but the mission buildings had been neglected and abandoned. It was used as the parish church for the city of San Gabriel. When the Claretian Mission Fathers arrived, they began the slow process of restoring the mission.

Soap Making

San Gabriel Arcangel supplied soap (and candles) to most of the California missions. The soap factory consisted of four large furnaces with a capacity of 2,686 gallons. Each furnace was a large brick-lined hole with edges lined in thick sheets of iron. A large iron pot sat in each furnace, with a fire burning beneath.

Like candle making, soap making was best done during the cold months. It was a long, hot, smelly job. Fat from cattle, sheep, hogs, and other animals was melted down into tallow and put in iron pots. Water was poured through wood ashes from fires to make a caustic liquid called lye. The liquid lye and melted fat were boiled in the iron kettles. As it cooled, the soft soap floated to the top and was skimmed off and poured into molds. It was cut into bars after it hardened. The new soap was stored on shelves and turned occasionally until it was thoroughly dried or "cured" and then was ready to be used. Today, the process is much safer and easier and can be made from many types of products. With the help of an adult, try making soap.

Use these precautions when making soap:

- Cover your work area with newspapers.

- Use stainless steel, iron, glass, or enameled pots. Do not use aluminum pots; they are ruined by lye.

- Use lye flakes (sometimes called caustic soda), *not* the type of lye used as a drain cleaner.

- Do not spill the lye; it can cause burns! If the lye touches your skin, wash the skin immediately with *cold* water and rinse with vinegar or lemon juice. Just to be safe, wear rubber gloves.

- Soft water works best. If the water is hard, add a ½ teaspoon (2 mL) lye flakes to the water at least 24 hours in advance, or use rainwater.

Activity

Directions

1. In a double boiler, melt 2½ pounds (1.134 kg) of tallow (animal fat).

2. In a separate pot, mix ¾ pint (375 mL) water into ½ of a 13-ounce (368.5-gram) can of lye.

3. Remove the double boiler from the stove. Slowly pour the lye mixture into the melted tallow. Stir very steadily, not too fast and not too slow. Keep mixing until the liquid turns thick and has the consistency of syrup, at least 15 minutes. If it gets lumpy, put the pot over the lowest heat and keep stirring until it becomes soft soap.

4. Pour it into a metal cookie tin, shallow pan, or shoe box that has been lined with waxed paper or plastic wrap. Let the mixture harden for at least 24 hours. Cut it into soap bars. It will still be soft, but after three to four more weeks, it will be ready to use.

San Fernando Rey de España Mission

City: Mission Hills
Founded: September 8, 1797
Order of founding: 17th
Founder: Padre Fermin Lasuen

San Fernando Rey de España became a convenient resting place between the San Buenaventura and San Gabriel missions. It was less than a day's travel from the rapidly growing pueblo of Los Angeles. The site was also the location of four springs, good land for agriculture, and friendly Indians.

The mission was successful from the beginning. On the day of its founding, ten Indian children were brought to be baptized. A small adobe church was completed on November 28, 1797. In 1799, a larger church was completed and buildings were started that would form the large quadrangle. In 1804, work was started on another church that was completed in 1806.

In 1812, an earthquake destroyed much of the third church. Although the church is interesting because of its blend of Moorish- and Spanish-style architecture, it is considered less interesting than some other missions, probably because it never had a great builder.

Many travelers stopped at San Fernando Rey de España. The padres' quarters were constantly being enlarged to accommodate these visitors. After 13 years, this "Convento" building reached a length of 243 feet (74 meters), the largest original structure remaining in the mission chain today. Visitors were housed and fed at no cost for as long as they wanted to stay. The building is famous for its 21 Roman arches. There are holes in the large mission doors where cats ran in and out chasing rats that ate the grain. The padres borrowed the cats from the San Gabriel Mission.

The mission was secularized in 1834. A group of young Californians wanted the mission lands. They led a series of uprisings. Governor Jose Maria Echeandia tried to convince the Indians that they shouldn't have to work at the missions. He equipped a small army of freed Indians to fight against a man who was running against him for governor. San Fernando became the headquarters of this short-lived revolt. Fighting ended when Echeandia was called back to Mexico.

The desire for mission lands grew even stronger in 1842 when gold was discovered on one of the San Fernando ranchos. Francisco Lopez, the ranch foreman of the mission, found gold on March 9, 1842 in what is now Placerita Canyon. This was the first documented incidence of California gold, six years before Marshall found gold at Sutter's Mill. An unknown early writer described the discovery stating, "Lopez, with a companion while in search of some stray horses, about midday stopped under some trees and tied their horses to feed. While resting in the shade, Lopez with his sheath knife dug up some wild onions, and in the dirt discovered a piece of gold. Searching further he found more. On his return to town he showed the pieces to his friends, who at once declared there must be a placer of gold there." In a few weeks, hundreds of people were seeking gold. For years, rumors continued about the gold. Treasure-seekers even dug up the floor of the abandoned church. They believed that gold had been buried there by the padres for their private use after mission days ended. After a few years, the excitement and the gold ran out, partly due to the much larger California Gold Rush that followed in 1848.

In 1845, the Mexican governor, Pio Pico, divided mission lands. He leased several thousand acres to his brother, Andres, for $1,120 a year. The governor then sold these lands to raise money to fight the Americans. Pico made San Fernando his headquarters in 1846. The buildings were sold by Pico just before California came under American control.

In 1851, U.S. Senator McClay and his partners bought the northern half of the rancho. The southern half had previously been sold to Isaac Lankershim, a land speculator. These two purchases ended the mission era and began the development of the town of San Fernando.

Although a small portion of the mission land was returned to the Catholic Church in a decree signed by Abraham Lincoln in 1862, there was little left that could be used. The mission was used as a warehouse and stable, its gardens became pigsties, and its roof tiles were taken for other buildings.

In 1896, the Landmarks Club launched a campaign to restore the buildings. On San Fernando Candle Day, 6,000 people bought candles at a dollar each to finance the purchase of a new roof. After dark they carried the flickering candles in a procession through the mission. Today its gardens and much of the quadrangle have been restored, but restoration has been ongoing. The 1971 Sylmar earthquake destroyed the fully restored church. In 1974, it was replaced with a replica of the 1806 church. The 1994 earthquake did additional damage.

Cattle Brands

Cattle raising was the most important industry at Mission San Fernando Rey de España. The mission got off to a good start because older missions gave the padres livestock. Many Indians were needed to herd, brand, guard, and slaughter the animals. In 1819, at the mission's peak, over 21,000 head of livestock grazed on its ranchos: 12,800 cattle, 7,800 sheep, 176 goats, 45 pigs, 780 horses, and 144 mules. Horses and mules were used for transportation. The churro breed of sheep was common at all of the missions. The coarse wool of these sheep was used to make blankets and clothes for the Indians.

Cattle herds were kept on ranchos away from the mission where there was grass for grazing and where they wouldn't destroy crops. Indian cowboys and their families often lived out on these ranchos to be near the herd.

Mission cattle sometimes strayed onto the lands of the Mexican settlers. In 1770, a Mexican decree required all cattle to be branded to show who owned them. Each mission had its own brand (special mark). Branding irons were heated in hot coals. The iron burned the brand into the flank of each animal. The branding was done at summer rodeos. Some cattle were butchered during rodeo time. Every part of the animal was used: beef was dried (or "jerked"), fat was saved for soap and candle making and for the tallow trade, Indians prepared smoked cattle tongues, and the rest of the cattle was left for the coyotes. Rodeos were also a time of great feasting, dancing, and showing off horsemanship skills.

Activity

Make a brand design out of a coat hanger.

1. On paper, draw a very simple design that represents *you*. Look at the mission brands chart to get ideas (page 34).
2. Remove cardboard that may be attached to your hanger.
3. Very carefully unwind a thin metal coat hanger. Then twist it into the brand design that you created on paper. Be careful not to poke yourself!
4. On a small piece of paper, write your name. Hang your name from the brand and display it for others to see.

   Note: You may also want to bend coat hangers to make the brands of the missions.

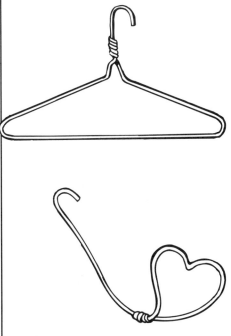

Cattle Brands of the California Missions

Mission	Brand
San Diego de Alcala	
San Luis Rey de Francia	
San Juan Capistrano	
San Gabriel Arcangel	
San Fernando Rey de España	
San Buenaventura	
Santa Barbara	
Santa Ines	
La Purisima Concepcion	
San Luis Obispo de Tolosa	
San Miguel Arcangel	

Mission	Brand
San Antonio de Padua	
Nuestra Señora de la Soledad	
San Carlos Borromeo del Carmelo	
San Juan Bautista	
Santa Cruz	
Santa Clara de Asis	
San Jose	
San Francisco de Asis	
San Rafael Arcangel	
San Francisco Solano	

San Buenaventura Mission

City: Ventura
Founded: March 31, 1782
Order of founding: 9th
Founder: Padre Junipero Serra

Padre Serra raised the cross to found San Buenaventura Mission on Easter Sunday. It was the ninth and last mission founded by Serra. After San Diego and Monterey, Serra had planned to build San Buenaventura as the third mission. Construction was delayed for 12 years due to Indian uprisings at other missions. There weren't enough soldiers to protect a new mission. Serra was also delayed because a new government policy made building new missions secondary to bringing Spanish settlers into Indian territory. Serra left Padre Benito Cambon in charge of the "Mission by the Sea."

The coastal area along the Santa Barbara channel had many Chumash Indian villages. The Chumash were skilled canoe builders and fishermen. An unknown diarist in 1769 wrote: "The handiness and ability of the Indians was at its best in the construction of their canoes. They handle these with skill, and in them three or four men go out to sea to fish, as they will hold eight or ten men. They use long double-bladed paddles and row with indescribable agility and swiftness." The women were known for the beautiful watertight reed baskets they wove. The Indians were very friendly and helped with the building of the mission. They lived in cone-shaped willow-thatched huts near the church.

The first church was destroyed by fire in 1791. A stone, adobe, and tile church was completed in 1809. Over the side door is a Moorish design. To the Chumash Indians, the design represented a map of the region. The upper line suggested the hills behind the mission. The curved lines stood for the Ventura and Santa Clara Rivers. The rivers flowed on each side of the mission, which was represented by the center cross.

An earthquake in 1812 forced the padres and Indians to seek temporary shelter a few miles inland. Many repairs were needed on the church. Although the upper parts of the church were nine feet (2.75 meters) "out of plumb," the padres decided to save the building. The walls were heavily buttressed to strengthen it against future earthquakes.

In 1818, a pirate, Hippolyte de Bouchard, was rumored to be pillaging missions in the area. Padre Jose Senan quickly gathered all mission valuables such as paintings, statues, vestments, and silver. These were buried or hidden in caves. The padres and Indians then took baskets of food and livestock into the hills, where they camped for about three weeks. They built a small chapel for temporary worship and waited for Bouchard to leave the area.

Soon after the padres and Indians returned to the mission, Mojave Indians arrived. They asked to see the padre, but the corporal locked the Mojaves in the guardhouse. The next morning, the angry Indians fought with the soldiers, and 13 people were killed. This event caused bad feelings among all the Indians. The Mojaves fled, but for months the mission lived in fear of a retaliation.

When secularization came in 1836, it was made easier because it was led by an honest administrator, Rafael Gonzales, but the inevitable decline occurred. In March 1838, a two-day battle was fought over the mission by the troops of rival candidates for governor, further damaging the crumbling mission buildings.

In 1845, San Buenaventura was rented to Jose Arnaz and Narcisco Botello. Then, on June 8, 1846, the mission and its lands were sold by the Mexican governor, Pio Pico, to Jose Arnaz for $12,000. Arnaz was perhaps California's first real estate promoter. He subdivided the town into lots and advertised them for sale to Americans in the East. He got no buyers, and Pico's sale was considered illegal by the United States government. After California became a U.S. state, the mission was returned to the Catholic Church by a proclamation by President Abraham Lincoln on May 23, 1862.

At the end of the last century, when the town experienced a railroad boom, Padre Rubio tried to "improve" the old mission to match the spirit of the times. His attempt at modernizing caused damage to the original building. The beamed ceiling was covered over; part of the quadrangle was razed; Indian artwork on the walls was whitewashed; a beautiful canopied pulpit of exquisite woodwork was removed; the tile floor was covered with wood; and the windows were enlarged and replaced with dark stained glass. Old photographs and drawings were used to restore the mission to its original form under the supervision of Father Aubrey J. O'Reilly from 1956–57.

Planting Crops from Seeds

Activity

Try growing a miniature orchard in your classroom. Growing plants from leftover fruit seeds will make nice houseplants, but will not mature into fruit-bearing trees. Fruit trees that grow in cooler climates, such as apples and pears, require a long chilling period before they sprout, so tropical fruit seeds are easier to grow.

To grow a citrus plant, follow these steps:

1. Remove seeds from the fruit. Soak the seeds in water for 24 hours.
2. Fill a pot with moist potting mix (nonsoil type). Plant the seeds ½-inch (1.25-cm) deep.
3. Keep seeds moist while they germinate. Germination will take about a month. They will grow well under fluorescent lights or on a windowsill.
4. When the plants grow about 12 inches (30.5 cm) tall, pinch back the top shoots to encourage bushy growth.

To grow a cool climate fruit plant, follow these steps:

1. Remove seeds from the fruit. Plant seeds ½-inch (1.25-cm) deep in moist sand or peat moss. Plant in pots or flats.
2. Put the containers in a cold garage or a refrigerator for three months.
3. Then follow Steps 2–4 under the citrus directions.

A reservoir and seven-mile-long clay pipe aqueduct provided water from the Ventura River to San Buenaventura Mission. With reliable water, good soil, and a pleasant climate, the mission grew abundant crops and large orchards. San Buenaventura became known for its apples, pears, peaches, pomegranates, grapes, grain, and olives. It also produced many exotic fruits such as bananas, sugar cane, figs, and coconuts. Sailing ships stopped at the mission to buy fresh produce. In 1793, an English navigator, Captain George Vancouver, was able to buy so many fruits and vegetables for his sailors that it took 20 pack mules to carry the produce to Santa Barbara, where his ship was anchored!

Santa Barbara Mission

City: Santa Barbara
Founded: December 4, 1786
Order of founding: 10th
Founder: Padre Fermin Lasuen

On April 21, 1782, Padre Serra blessed the founding of the Santa Barbara Presidio and its chapel, thinking that permission for a nearby mission would come soon. He was not aware that Governor Felipe de Neve would not give permission. The governor thought that the missions had too much economic power. Governor Neve thought that there should be just one padre instead of two at Santa Barbara, instead of the way the other nine missions were organized. The padre should live next to a chapel with a few soldiers to guard him. Instead of teaching in a mission, the padre should visit the Indian villages and teach them about Christianity there. The governor wanted this plan approved by the king of Spain before more missions were built in Alta California. Serra fought against the plan. He waited three weeks, expecting to receive permission to start the mission, but then sadly returned to his headquarters at Carmel. He died a month after receiving word from a new governor, Pedro Fages, that permission was granted to build the Santa Barbara mission and to organize it like the other nine.

Padre de Lasuen dedicated this new mission on the Feast of St. Barbara, December 4, 1786. The mission was dedicated again on December 16th, when the new governor was able to attend. Padre de Lasuen left Padres Antonio Paterna and Cristobal Oramas to run the mission. The first temporary buildings were built in log-cabin style. As more Indians came to live at the mission, larger adobe churches were built in 1789 and 1794. An 1812 earthquake severely damaged the church, so a new stone church was started in 1815. This new church was planned by Father Antonio Ripoll. The architectural style combined Greek, Roman, Spanish, Moorish, and Indian influences. In 27 B.C., a Roman architect named Vitruvius Polion wrote *The Six Books of Architecture*, which was published and republished in Europe through the centuries. A Spanish translation eventually turned up in the mission library. Ripoll admired Vitruvius Polion's work and built the façade of the Santa Barbara mission from details found in the book. It took five years for the Mexican stonemason, Jose Ramirez, and his Indian helpers to build the church. Santa Barbara is the only mission with twin towers. A huge celebration was held when the church was completed in 1820. There was a fiesta with food, music, bullfights, and fireworks. Mission Santa Barbara is known as the "Queen of the Missions" because of its elegant design and beautiful location near the ocean.

The Chumash and Canaliño Indians of the Santa Barbara area welcomed the Spanish. They helped build the churches, plant and harvest crops, and work at crafts and industry and were known for their music. Padre Narciso Duran was famous for his mission music. He trained a group of Indian musicians and wrote several masses that are still sung in the mission church. He was also known for a Christmas play that he produced each year.

On February 21, 1824, an Indian rider arrived with news that a soldier at Santa Ines Mission had beaten an Indian without good reason. The Indians at Santa Ines were fighting against the Spanish. The Indians at Santa Barbara joined the fight because they felt that the soldiers punished them too harshly. The padres at both missions made them work hard, daily life was strict, and Indians were dying from new illnesses. After the fighting stopped, the Indians escaped into the hills. Only a few Indians stayed behind. Work at the mission nearly stopped. Padres Vicente de Sarria and Ripoll visited the Indians and urged them to return. Many eventually returned, but some decided they never wanted to go back.

The Santa Barbara Mission was secularized in 1834, but Padre Duran, then presidente of the missions, moved his headquarters here. Also, Francisco Garcia Diego, first bishop of California, chose Santa Barbara as his headquarters. This prevented the plunder that ruined other missions and tended to keep the Mexican government away. Then, in 1846, both of these men died within a month of each other.

The Mexican governor, Pio Pico, tried to sell the mission and keep the money for himself. This sale was invalidated when United States troops arrived. Franciscan priests were sent from St. Louis, Missouri to run the mission. Santa Barbara is the only mission that has always had a Franciscan padre living there to look after the buildings. Inside the church is an altar light that has burned continuously for over 150 years!

Even though the mission wasn't destroyed, there was earthquake damage, especially in 1925. Californians raised $400,000 to restore the beautiful church. By 1927, the front of the church and towers were rebuilt in the original design. Later, cracks developed due to chemical disintegration of the concrete used in the repairs. The front of the church was so weakened that it had to be taken down and rebuilt again with steel-reinforced concrete in 1950.

From 1868 until 1877, the Franciscans ran a high school and junior college for boys. A seminary was opened at the mission in 1896 for boys studying for the priesthood. Today, the mission church is used as a parish church.

Aqueduct: Water Movement

The Santa Barbara mission had the most complete water system of any mission. The elaborate system of dams, reservoirs, and aqueducts was well engineered. Water came from creeks and runoff in the hills behind the mission. A two-mile-long stone aqueduct took the water to two storage reservoirs that had been dammed by sandstone rocks. There was a settling tank to clear the silt from the water and a water-powered gristmill to grind flour. From the reservoirs, the water continued through aqueducts to the mission kitchen, hospital, fountain, laundry, gardens, corrals, fields, and orchards.

Some of this water flowed into a large, ornate, Moorish-style fountain that was built in front of the monastery wing in 1808. Overflow from the fountain came through the mouth of a carved stone bear into a 7-foot-long (2.25-meter) stone wash basin called a lavendaria, where Indian women washed their clothes. The sloped sides of the basin were used to beat soaped clothes with wooden paddles. The clean clothes were then rinsed in the basin.

Although the water system was originally built by the padres and Indians, parts of it are still used by the city water system, over 200 years later! Today the mission dam can be seen in Santa Barbara's Botanical Garden near the mission.

The Santa Barbara mission's water system used the principle of gravity to move water downhill. Gravity is one of the forces that control how the physical world works. It attempts to pull things toward the center of the earth. To demonstrate this in a sink, pour water into a container that has been turned on its side and propped up at a 45-degree angle. Let it fill with water and then overflow, creating a waterfall. The waterfall flows downward, rather than upward, due to the force of gravity.

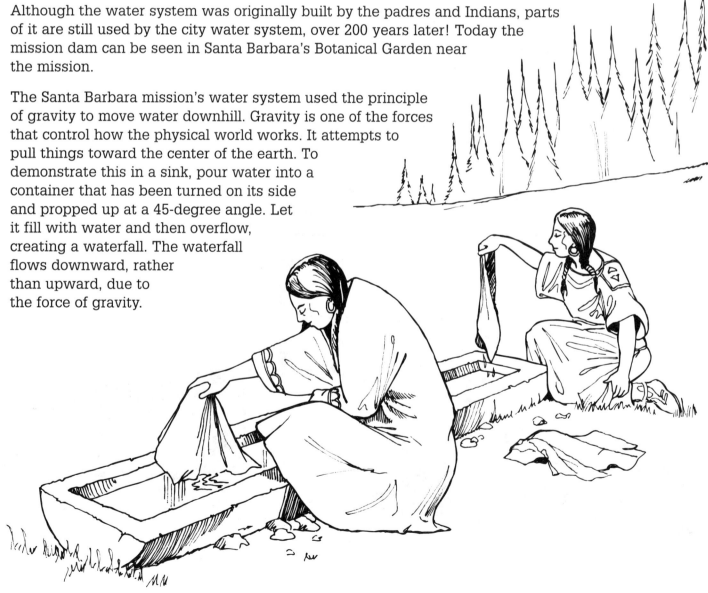

40

Aqueduct: Water Movement

Activity

Most of today's water systems are more sophisticated than the gravity-driven downhill system at Santa Barbara. Now, water even flows uphill! To demonstrate a very simple way to show water movement, try this experiment. You will need a basin of water, two clear drinking glasses, food coloring, and about 12 inches (30.5 cm) of clear plastic tubing (about ¼-inch [6.25 cm] in diameter, from a hardware store).

1. Place one empty glass on a table. Next to it place a glass filled with water that has a small amount of food coloring added to make the water seen more easily.

2. Submerge the tubing in the basin of water. Fill the tube with water and place fingers over both ends so that no water escapes. Quickly submerge one end of the tubing into the glass full of water. Put the other end into the bottom of the empty glass. Water will immediately begin flowing from the filled glass to the empty glass, stopping when the water levels are even in both glasses.

3. Raise one of the glasses 2–3 inches (5–7.5 cm) by holding it or putting it on a stack of books. The flow will start again from the higher glass to the lower glass until the water levels are even. Then, raise the lower glass and the flow will instantly reverse, stopping when the water levels are even. Try this many times. You will see that the water always flows from the higher level to the lower level and always stops once the levels (not necessarily the amount) of water in the two glasses match.

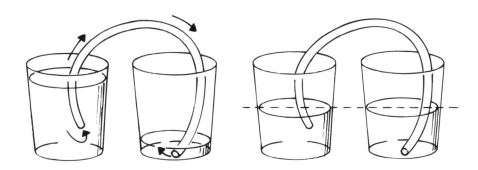

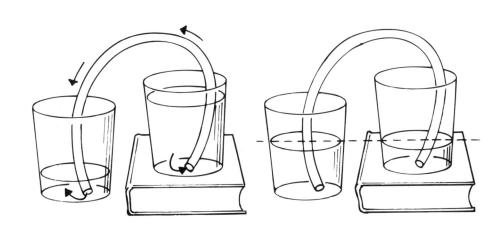

Juana Maria

Before sea otter hunters arrived, one of California's Channel Islands, San Nicolas, supported a large Indian population. However, when the hunters came to kill the otters for their fur, many Indians were killed and their way of life was changed forever. In 1835, the padres at Santa Barbara asked an American sea captain to visit the island and bring the 25 remaining Indians to the mission. When the Indians realized that the sailors were there to help, they accepted the offer. The ship arrived during a storm so they had to leave quickly.

Once the Indians were on the ship, a young mother began to search frantically for her lost baby. When she discovered that it had been left behind, she pleaded with the captain to return to the island. The storm made this too dangerous. The captain said he would return the next day if the storm had passed, but that didn't satisfy the mother, who didn't want to leave her baby among the wild dogs on the island for even one night. The mother jumped overboard to swim back to the island. The crew saw her disappear from sight in the dangerous waters and thought that she had drowned. No ships were available to return in the next few weeks, and it was assumed that even if she had survived the swim, it would have been very difficult to remain alive on the island with no one else to help her.

Fifteen years later, sea otter hunters stopped at the island. The padres had told them the tale of the woman, and they agreed to look for signs of what might have happened to her. They saw evidence that people had lived there after the Indians left, but it didn't appear that anyone was still alive. Their stories created a lot of excitement, and soon another hunting group arrived, but saw no one. As they left during a storm, a sailor was astounded to see the figure of a woman standing on a ridge. When it disappeared from sight, they thought that it might have been a ghost.

The woman truly was alive. She had kept herself hidden for 18 years, remembering the original, cruel hunters. Sadly, she had never been able to find her baby. She put all her survival skills to work, finding food, building shelter, and making clothes entirely from cormorant feathers. She had found two puppies abandoned by a pack of wild dogs. Even though they were wild, they responded to her kindness and became companions.

Soon a third group of hunters arrived on the island and found her. They convinced her they were just there to help and she left with them. She was warmly welcomed at Mission Santa Barbara and treated kindly with respect and gifts. She was given the name Juana Maria. However, she soon became ill and died. A plaque on a cemetery wall at the mission honors her remarkable survival:

Juana Maria
Indian woman abandoned on San Nicolas Island for eighteen years was found and brought back to Santa Barbara by Capt. George Nidever in 1853.

Today, San Nicolas Island, once the site of sea otter hunting, is the site of a sea otter breeding colony, helping to ensure their survival.

The popular fiction book *Island of the Blue Dolphins* by Scott O'Dell is based on the story of Juana Maria's life.

Display of Juana Maria's Life

Activity

Imagine that you are the curator of the Vatican Museum in the 1830s. As the curator, you are in charge of the museum. You must design the exhibits that tell the story of the amazing life of Juana Maria. By yourself or with others, design a real exhibit (display) of what Juana Maria's life might have been like, including life on the island and at the mission. Your exhibit must include both displays and written information.

The following list may provide possible ideas for your exhibit:

- Maps

- Sketches

- Interactive displays in which the viewer actually does something

- Paragraph descriptions

- Photographs

- Three-dimensional models that the viewer observes

- Tape recordings or video production

- Music

- Dioramas

After Juana Maria died in 1835 at the Santa Barbara mission, the story of her survival reached all the way to the Vatican in Rome, Italy, the world headquarters of the Catholic Church. One of the feathered garments she made out of cormorant feathers was displayed in the Vatican Museum.

Santa Ines Mission

City: Solvang
Founded: September 17, 1804
Order of founding: 19th
Founder: Padre Estevan Tapis

Santa Ines was founded by Padre Estevan Tapis, who succeeded Padre de Lasuen after his death in 1803. The mission was located in the beautiful, isolated valley of the Santa Ines River. In 1804, the other missions were at their height, so they were able to offer help. Local Indians had heard about missions, and 200 Indians came to watch the founding and to present 27 children for baptism. Although there were many Indians in the area, the neophyte population never grew above 768, which was smaller than the padres had imagined.

The mission expanded rapidly. An adobe church was completed within a year, a convento building was added as a wing, and soon other buildings were built to form the standard mission quadrangle. Some of the construction was done by Joseph Chapman, a Boston sailor, who once worked for the pirate Hippolyte de Bouchard. "Pirate Joe" was captured and sentenced to be executed. According to legend, his life was spared by the pleadings of the Maria Guadalupe, daughter of Don Ortega, whose ranch he had pillaged. Chapman was paroled to Santa Ines and baptized a Catholic at San Buenaventura, where he led a respectable life. He apparently could fix anything and became a general handyman at Santa Ines, where he built the gristmill. Maria Guadalupe Ortega, the rancher's daughter, broke her arm, and Chapman was able to set it. The grateful rancher offered Chapman anything he wanted, and Chapman chose the daughter! They were married at the mission.

Santa Ines was built to serve the Indians on the other side of the coastal mountains from Santa Barbara. Their tallow industry, woodwork, and leather work were well known. Santa Ines was located off the main travel routes, so it was a lonely place to live. Visitors were rare, but were greeted with ringing bells and a joyous welcome.

The mission started well, but soon had difficulties. Almost as soon as building was complete, the 1812 earthquake destroyed most of the church and many other buildings. Rebuilding started in 1813 under the guidance of Padre Francisco Javier de Uria, and a new church was dedicated in 1817.

In 1824, an Indian revolt strained relations with the Spanish and Indians. The problem started in 1810, when Mexico became independent from Spain. The government no longer provided pay for the soldiers or money to run the missions. The missions had to support the soldiers. The Indians were resentful of the hard work that it took to support the idle soldiers, who were often abusive and unkind to the Indians. The Indians revolted February 21, 1824, when a Santa Ines soldier beat a neophyte for a minor infraction. The Indians rebelled, but their weapons couldn't compete with the soldiers' guns. Some of the Indians were killed and fire burned much of the mission. When the Indians saw the roof of the church on fire, they helped put it out because their argument was with the soldiers, not the padres; but relations were never the same. The rebelling Indians fled to Santa Barbara and La Purisima, where more fighting took place.

Order was finally restored at Santa Ines. Buildings were repaired and rebuilt between 1825 and 1832. Secularization hit the mission hard in 1834. In 1836, Governor Chico "granted" the mission to Jose Covarrubias, who rented it for $580 a year. He moved his family into half of the building, and the padres kept the half containing the church. There was a dispute about the use of the quadrangle. To avoid future troubles, the "Father's Wall" was built down the middle. During this period, the Indians gradually left the mission.

In 1843, the management of the mission was returned to the padres, but it never regained its former prosperity. Total ruin never occurred because a friendly governor, Micheltorrena, granted nearly 36,000 acres of land to the first bishop of California for the establishment of a seminary in 1843. This became the College of our Lady of Refuge, the first college in the future state of California. It was later moved to College Ranch, where it operated until 1881.

In 1846, Santa Ines was sold for $7,000. That same year, the United States seized California and the sale was invalidated. Some property was later returned to the church.

Although Santa Ines was never completely abandoned, it did fall into disrepair. Regular maintenance was neglected. One Sunday in the 1860s, the pulpit collapsed under the astonished padre while he was preaching! In an 1862 decree, President Abraham Lincoln restored Santa Ines to the Catholic Church. Over the years, various families and padres lived at the mission and helped with the repair and reconstruction process.

Graphing Livestock

Activity

In 1832, two years before secularization, the missions were at the height of their development. The following livestock count is from December 31, 1832. Using the chart below, create a bar graph that makes some type of comparison. Here are some possibilities:

- Difference in the number of one type of animal between each mission, such as the number of horses each mission owns
- Difference in the number of animals at any one mission, such as number of cattle, sheep, goats, and so on

All missions raised crops and livestock to feed the padres, Indians, and soldiers. Santa Ines Mission was famous for its large herds of cattle and rich crops. The government required the padres to write a report each year telling how the mission was doing. The presidente of all the California missions had them keep track of the amount of crops and livestock and the number of births, baptisms, marriages, and deaths. A comparison of the mission records gives an interesting look at the success of each mission and of the total mission chain.

Mission	Cattle	Sheep	Goats	Swine	Horses	Mules	Total
San Diego de Alcala	4,500	13,250	150		220	80	18,200
San Luis Rey de Francia	27,500	26,100	1,300	300	1,950	180	57,330
San Juan Capistrano	10,900	4,800	50	40	450	30	16,270
San Gabriel Arcangel	16,500	8,500	40	60	1,200	42	26,342
San Fernando Rey de España	7,000	1,000			1,000	60	9,060
San Buenaventura	4,050	3,000	16	290	200	60	7,616
Santa Barbara	1,800	3,200	28	64	480	135	5,707
Santa Ines	7,200	2,100		60	390	110	9,860
La Purisima Concepcion	9,200	3,500	20	65	1,000	200	13,985
San Luis Obispo de Tolosa	2,500	5,422			700	200	8,822
San Miguel Arcangel	3,710	8,282	42	50	700	186	12,970
San Antonio de Padua	6,000	10,500	65	70	774	82	17,491
Nuestra Señora de la Soledad	6,000	6,200			252	56	12,508
San Carlos Borromeo del Rio Carmelo	2,100	3,300			410	8	5,818
San Juan Bautista	6,000	6,004		20	296	13	12,333
Santa Cruz	3,600	5,211			400	25	9,236
Santa Clara de Asis	10,000	9,500		55	730	35	20,320
San Jose	12,000	11,000		40	1,100	40	24,180
San Francisco de Asis	5,000	3,500			1,000	18	9,518
San Rafael Arcangel	2,120	3,000			370	2	5,492
San Francisco Solano	3,500	600		50	900	13	5,063
TOTAL	151,180	137,969	1,711	1,164	14,522	1,575	308,121

La Purisima Concepcion Mission

City: Lompoc
Founded: December 8, 1787
Order of founding: 11th
Founder: Padre Fermin de Lasuen

Padre de Lasuen dedicated the first site of La Purisima mission in today's Lompoc on December 8, 1787, but building wasn't started until after the rainy season the next spring. It was first built of wood poles plastered with mud and later replaced with adobe buildings. On its 25th anniversary, December 8, 1812, La Purisima was shaken by an earthquake. On December 21, the mission was completely destroyed by another series of quakes. Heavy rain and a flood further hampered the mission. Ten days after the earthquake, Padre Payeras wrote in his annual report: "We shall go to work constructing of poles and grass what is indispensable until the earth becomes quiet. Experience may teach us the best method of constructing other buildings." The next year, the padres and Indians rebuilt the mission four miles to the northeast.

The long, narrow church was large enough to hold all of the mission's residents, including a thousand Indian neophytes. There were no benches in the mission churches. People sat or knelt on the floor during the services. Men were seated on one side and women on the other, separated by a line down the center. Bells called people to services twice each day. The services were given in Latin, Spanish, or the native Chumash. The commonly used language of the mission was probably a combination of Chumash and Spanish.

La Purisima thrived under the 19-year leadership of Padre Mariano Payeras. He was loved and respected. When he became presidente of all the missions in 1815, he chose to stay at La Purisima, and this mission became the headquarters of the California mission system. Payeras improved the mission's water supply and irrigation system, so food production increased. He is buried under the altar at La Purisima.

La Purisima had some difficult years. It suffered during a severe drought in the winter of 1816–1817, when hundreds of sheep died of hunger. Then fire destroyed nearly all of the neophytes' homes in 1818. Their beloved Padre Payeras died in 1823.

The Indians at La Purisima also rebelled when they heard about the revolt against cruel soldiers at Santa Ines in 1824. They fortified the buildings and held the mission in siege for a month. When the governor heard of the crisis, he sent 109 soldiers from the presidio at Monterey to fight the Indians. The Indians' weapons were no match for those of the soldiers. In two and a half hours the Indians had to give up. Sixteen Indians and one soldier were killed. The padres were saddened when seven Indian leaders were executed and 12 others were jailed.

It was hard for the mission to return to normal after the revolt. The defeat was hard on the Indians' pride, and many of them did return to the mission.

Within ten years the mission was secularized. The mission lands were sold by the Mexican governor, Pio Pico, for $1,100 to Juan Temple of Los Angeles in 1845. Over the years, the buildings were passed from owner to owner. As the buildings decayed through neglect and weathering, they were used as barns for cattle and sheep, and part of the mission was even used as a saloon. The site was returned to the church in 1874, but was sold because of its dilapidated condition.

The Union Oil Company acquired most of the land in 1903 and donated it so that the mission could be restored. In 1933, the mission was given to Santa Barbara County. In 1934, control was turned over to the California Department of Parks and Recreation for restoration. Only part of the walls and a few pillars were still standing. Historians, archaeologists, engineers, and architects spent nearly a year studying the mission's original structure in order to recreate life in the 1820s. Under the supervision of the National Park Service, State Park Commission, and a distinguished advisory committee, the Civilian Conservation Corps (CCC) rebuilt and furnished much of the mission between 1934 and 1941. They used original tools and methods whenever possible. The buildings look authentic, but hidden within the adobe walls are modern building technologies for protection against earthquakes.

The state took great pains to reproduce all parts of the mission, including the gardens. The gardens contain a wide variety of plants that were used by the Indians and padres for food, fiber, and medicine. There are both native plants and many species introduced by the padres. Pomegranates, figs, pears, pepper trees, grapevines, and Castillian roses now grow here but were started from grafts or cuttings taken from plants at other California missions.

The grounds also have livestock from the correct genetic types from mission years. The four-horned "churro" sheep and longhorn cattle, for example, are descended from those brought to the Southwest by the Spanish. Over the years, the park area has been enlarged to keep the look of mission times and to keep modern buildings out of view. Volunteers dress in clothes like those worn in the 1820s, give tours, and demonstrate crafts such as weaving and candle making.

Dipping Candles

La Purisima Concepcion mission had an outside tallow rendering center. Tallow is the liquefied fat of any animal. Large chunks of animal fat were melted and purified in these vats. This "rendered" tallow was then stored in cowhide bags to be traded to American ships and other missions or to be used at the mission for cooking and making candles and soap.

Before electric lights and gas lamps, candles were used for lighting. Candles of tallow were the most common type used at the missions. They were made by the Indians, who boiled and stirred tallow in huge iron kettles. One method of making candles used a candle rack. Pieces of string were hung from the rack. Each time the rack was lowered into the melted fat, layers of tallow built up on the string, making the candles thicker. After each dipping, the strings were pulled out so the fat could cool and harden. This was repeated many times until the candles reached the desired thickness. The candles were then cut from the rack and stored or traded. They had to be stored carefully so they wouldn't break or become a meal for mice.

Dipping Candles

Activity

Enjoy making your own candles, but do it with the help of an adult. Paraffin is very flammable. Keep baking soda handy as a fire extinguisher in case the wax should come in contact with a flame.

Materials

- Cotton string or store-bought candlewicks
- Paraffin wax (available at grocery stores)
- Wooden spoon and heavy knife
- Potholder
- Coffee can (size that will fit into the saucepan)
- Saucepan filled ⅔ full of water
- Double boiler
- Newspaper
- Optional: alum or stearin for hardening candles
- Optional for colored candles: crayons or lipstick stubs

Directions

1. Cut a length of string twice as long as the depth of the coffee can.

2. Set up the double boiler. (Do NOT place a saucepan of wax directly on a burner without the double boiler!)

3. Fill the saucepan ⅔ full of water.

4. Cut paraffin into small pieces and place inside the coffee can. (You can also add pieces of old candles.)

5. Place the coffee can into the saucepan. It cannot float.

6. Melt the paraffin over medium heat, but don't overheat it; it could ignite. You can add either stearic acid or alum during the melting stage in order to harden the fat. The candle will last longer, and dripping is eliminated. Use one part stearin to ten parts paraffin. These hardeners are available at a pharmacy or craft store.

7. If you want the candle to be a color other than white, add pieces of crayon or lipstick stubs to the melted paraffin. Stir them into the wax until the color is even.

8. Hold the string in the middle so that two strands hang down. This will allow you to make two candles at a time. You can also tie pieces of string to a pencil or stick and dip several at a time.

9. Dip the two ends of the string into the melted paraffin. Pull them out. Hold them straight and let the wax harden for about a minute, being careful not to drip wax on anything important. Holding them over newspaper works well. Repeat the process until the candles are the size you want.

10. If you want to make candle wax in a more traditional way, rather than buying paraffin, follow these steps:

Get fat from a butcher. You need about 2 pounds (907 g) of tallow for a dozen candles. Cut the fat into ½-inch (1.25-cm) chunks. Melt it in a large, heavy pan over low heat, with a small amount of water. You can speed up the process by pressing the fat with the back of a slotted spoon or a potato masher.

Stir constantly so any particles that settle will not scorch. When cracklings (fibers around which fat clings) rise to the top, scoop them out. Spread muslin or cheesecloth in a wire sieve. When the fat is liquefied and still fairly warm, remove it from the heat. Strain the lard by pouring it through the cloth and sieve into a deep container. If you won't be making candles from the tallow right away, store it in the refrigerator. Boil cotton string to remove additives, soak in vinegar, and let it dry. Twist the string into wicks. Then follow directions for making candles.

San Luis Obispo de Tolosa Mission

City: San Luis Obispo
Founded: September 1, 1772
Order of founding: 5th
Founder: Padre Junipero Serra

In 1772, Padre Serra received news that two ships loaded with supplies were in San Diego and would not sail any farther because of stormy weather. Serra needed the supplies for the missions. He and Governor Fages traveled to San Diego to convince the ship captains to sail north to Monterey.

Serra had started the San Luis Obispo mission on his way to San Diego, in an area where Governor Fages had hunted bears and given bear meat to the Indians. The area was named "Valley of the Bears" by Gaspar de Portola in December 1769 on his unsuccessful trip to find Monterey Bay.

Eight-foot (2.5-meter) tall, 1,200-pound (544-kg) grizzly bears were hard to kill, but the starving men of the mission appreciated the meat. Bear meat later saved the lives of starving people from other missions. In 1772, over 9,000 pounds (4,082 kg) of salted and jerked bear meat was taken to the starving people at Missions San Carlos Borromeo del Rio Carmelo and San Antonio de Padua. They also took 25 mule loads of edible seeds that they had gotten from trading bear meat with the Indians.

In 1772, Serra left Padre Jose Cavaller, five soldiers, and two neophytes to build the mission. He left very few supplies: flour, chocolate, wheat for sowing, and brown sugar to trade with the Indians for seeds. Cavaller and his men survived only with the help of generous Indians.

The first mission was made of wood poles and tree boughs but was later replaced with adobe buildings. The present church was completed in 1793, and most of the priests' quarters were finished in 1794.

In the beginning, the Chumash Indians found little to interest them at the mission. They were friendly because they remembered how Governor Fages had helped rid their valley of dangerous grizzly bears and given them bear meat to eat. Food often drew Indians to the missions. At San Luis Obispo de Tolosa, the Indians began to come when crops of corn and beans were planted. The mission was known for its fine olive groves, orchards, and vineyards. The first olive trees in California were planted at San Luis Obispo de Tolosa.

Although it was usual practice to have two padres at each mission, Padre Cavaller served alone for the first 17 years. After he died, Padre Luis Antonio Martinez came to San Luis Obispo de Tolosa. His friendliness, generosity, and humor brought many Indians to the mission. Padre Martinez became a legendary figure. In 1818, Padre Martinez left his sick bed to lead a group of neophytes to battle the pirate, Hippolyte de Bouchard, in Santa Barbara and San Juan Capistrano. They never got the chance to fight Bouchard, but the adventure added to his legendary status.

Once, Martinez staged a "poultry parade" to entertain guests General Moreno and his new bride. This scene is described in the novel *Ramona*. Martinez "caused to be driven past the corridors for their inspection, all the poultry belonging to the mission. The procession took an hour to pass. It would be safe to say that a droller sight never was seen, and never will be on the Pacific Coast or any other."

The Chumash Indians at San Luis Obispo de Tolosa seemed happy. They did not want to join the uprisings like those at Santa Ines, Santa Barbara, and La Purisima. However, their happiness did not last, because Padre Martinez was arrested. The outspoken padre was not appreciated by some government officials. Officials falsely accused him of taking money and killing mission cattle. He was given an illegal court-martial and forced to return to Spain by Governor Jose Echeandia in 1830 after 34 years of service at the mission.

At the time of secularization, the property was valued at $70,000, but within a few years it was worth almost nothing. Indians drove off livestock, settlers claimed some of the land, and the buildings deteriorated. In 1845, the Mexican governor, Pio Pico, sold everything except the church for $510. Over the years, some rooms were used as a jail and as a courthouse. The chapel and some of the land was returned to the Catholic Church after the United States government took over in 1846.

Attempts were made to restore the mission as early as 1847 by Padre Garcia. The mission went through several architectural changes, such as enclosing it in wood siding and adding a bell steeple. San Luis Obispo de Tolosa became a parish church after secularization.

A fire in 1920 exposed the original style of the building. Serious restoration began in 1935, and by 1947, the mission was restored to its 1794 look. Mission Plaza has been built in front of the church and is the town center for San Luis Obispo. Although there are no longer bear- and bullfights like there were in the 1860s, the area is still filled with activity.

Making Tiles for Roofs

Indians from the south were not as friendly as the Chumash mission Indians. The mission was attacked three times by enemies of the neophytes who lived there. In 1776, 1778, and 1782, hostile Indians shot burning arrows into the dry tule-thatched roofs, setting the mission on fire. To make the buildings less likely to be burned, the missionaries started covering their roofs with curved tiles. The tiles also helped protect the adobe walls from erosion due to rain and kept the interior of the buildings dry.

The padres remembered the red roof tiles, or tejas, from Spain and began to experiment with the best way to manufacture them. The clay was worked in pits, with horse and burro hooves kneading it until it was soft enough to mold. The tiles were made from the same clay as adobe bricks, but they had less sand. The clay mixture was put into flat molds and then removed from the molds when they were still wet. Clay rectangles were molded over curved wooden forms. (It has been said that Indian women molded tiles over their legs, but this is not true.) After the edges were trimmed, tiles dried in the sun and baked for a long time in wood-burning kilns. The slow baking of these tiles made them red, long-lasting, and fireproof.

It is often said that San Luis Obispo de Tolosa was the first mission to use tile roofing. However, Serra wrote to Padre Lasuen, crediting Mission San Antonio de Padua with being the first to make and use the tiles. Regardless of which mission was actually first, the tile roofs were so successful that by 1784, all of the missions had adopted the new method of roofing. This popular architectural style is now found throughout California and the Southwest.

Activity

Using red modeling clay, form miniature roof tiles.

Directions

1. Form the clay into an approximate 3" x 4" (7.5 cm x 10 cm) flat rectangular shape.

2. Mold clay over a toilet paper tube to get the half-round shape. Allow to dry.

3. Make at least five clay tiles. Arrange the tiles in the sequence used on many of the tile roofs.

4. Although regular modeling clay won't keep its shape like fired clay, it will show how tiles were made and how long it took to create enough for all the mission buildings.

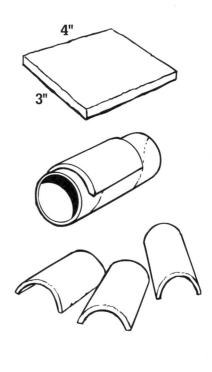

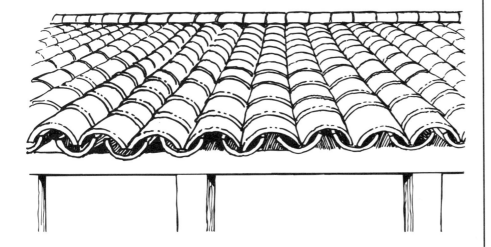

San Miguel Arcangel Mission

City: San Miguel
Founded: July 25, 1797
Order of founding: 16th
Founder: Padre Fermin de Lasuen

Padre de Lasuen founded San Miguel Arcangel halfway between San Luis Obispo and San Antonio de Padua. It was located in a fertile valley near the Nacimiento and Salinas Rivers. Padre Buenaventura Sitjar was put in charge. On the founding day, 15 Salinan Indian youth were baptized. The Indians near the mission were friendly, but the padres had less success with attracting the more hostile Tulare Indians from the San Joaquin Valley.

Although at first the mission went smoothly with the Indians, there was difficulty with Padre Sitjar's assistant, Padre Antonio de la Concepcion Horra. The heat and many ants and termites bothered him. It was said that even the flies and fleas died in the heat, gasping for breath! Padre Antonio started doing strange things like firing off guns that scared away some of the Indians. He went insane and was sent back to Mexico.

One month after the mission was founded, Padre Juan Martin came to take Padre Antonio's place. Martin stayed for 27 years. He became the great builder of San Miguel Arcangel and mastered the Salinan Indian language.

Several simple churches were built in the first few years. A terrible fire in 1806 destroyed half of the church's roof. Storerooms of wool, cloth, leather goods, and over 6,000 bushels of wheat were also destroyed. This was a tremendous loss. If it hadn't been for the generous donations of food, clothing, and equipment from nearby missions, people at San Miguel Arcangel would not have survived. Within a year, the mission was functioning again. The land holdings of the mission were large. The pastures, fields, and orchards stretched 50 miles to the north and south of the mission. Like some of the missions, San Miguel Arcangel had small ranchos miles from the mission, where Indians were in charge of tending the fields and livestock.

Work on a new church was started in 1816. The Indians had begun making adobe bricks, floor tile, and roof tile for the new church many years earlier. They cut and hauled 44-foot-long (13.5-meter) roof timbers from pine forests many miles away. Because of the previous work making bricks and tiles, it only took two years to build the church, but the roof took another year. The San Miguel mission Indians became so good at making roof tiles that they were known for trading them with other missions. Between 1808 and 1809, they made 36,000 tiles!

In 1831, Jose Echeandia, the first governor sent from Mexico, decreed that the missions must free any Indians who wanted to leave. Through an interpreter, Jose Castro, the new local commissioner, asked all the Indians who wished to have freedom to stand on his left side and those who wished to stay with the padre to stand to the right. Most of the Indians chose to stay with the padre. The governor's decree was not enforced, but in 1834, the mission was secularized. The mission was confiscated and all the property was distributed among the Indians. Within a few years, the Indian population was down to a few hundred, with few livestock left.

On July 4, 1846, the Mexican governor, Pio Pico, transferred ownership of mission buildings to William Reed and Petronillo Rios. This transfer took place just three days before Commodore Sloat of the U.S. Navy sailed into the harbor at Monterey.

William Reed moved his family and their household help into an entire wing of the mission. They lived there for years, disputing the claim that the sale was illegal. Travelers often stopped for several days at the old mission to rest.

On December 4, 1848, five unsavory men arrived. Reed invited them for dinner and unwisely bragged about the money he had made from selling cattle, sheep, and gold that he had brought back from the gold fields. The men pretended to continue their journey and then doubled back and attacked. The would-be thieves killed ten people—Reed, his wife, children, servants, and visitors. They literally tore the building apart in an attempt to find gold. When they found none, they fled. A posse caught up with the murderers on the oceanside cliffs near Santa Barbara. In a bloody fight, one robber was killed and another leaped into the ocean and drowned. The other three were captured and taken to Santa Barbara, where they were promptly tried, convicted, and shot. Ever since, there have been legends of ghosts prowling the ruins at the mission.

In 1859, the property was returned to the Catholic Church by a decree of President Buchanan. Since the church had no pastor between 1842 and 1878, it is surprising that the interior remained in its original condition. Over the years, a tavern, dance hall, general store, and Howe sewing-machine store rented space for their businesses.

In 1928, the mission was returned to the Franciscans, and extensive restorations began. Today it is a parish church with an extensive garden, displaying many varieties of cacti.

Stenciling Patterns

As the San Miguel Arcangel church was nearing completion, Padre Martin wrote to his artist friend, Esteban Munras of Monterey. Munras was asked to help the Indians paint designs on the church walls. Munras was a childhood friend of Padre Martin. They both came from the same part of Catalonia, Spain. Munras agreed to decorate the church as a favor.

From ancient pattern books of Greek and Roman architecture, Munras found designs and pictures he liked and added his interpretation of the bright colors. They were used to complement the bright colors of Mexican decorations. Materials for painting were either imported or were found locally. The pigments were almost all made from minerals, except black from charcoal or soot and some blue from indigo. No colors were made from flowers because their colors faded quickly. Reds came from iron ores or cinnabar; brilliant vermillion, carmine, and orange had to be imported. Yellows and browns came from ochres, and green from copper ore. Blue came from copper sulphate and cobalt aluminate. The pigments were in a powder form, with cactus juice added as a liquid to make the colors last for years. Brushes were imported in the early years, but later had to be made of locally available materials.

For many months in 1821, Munras and the Indians painted designs, pictures of doorways and balconies, and even an elaborate reredos with an All-Seeing-Eye of God blazing above a statue of St. Michael. Since they were not damaged by weather, vandals, or restorers, these artworks look as fresh as when they were first painted. Except for some careful retouching of missing parts in the 1930s, the paintings are like they were originally. These are the best preserved original decorations of any California mission.

Almost all wall surfaces to be painted were whitewashed first. Designs were scratched into the whitewashed surface with a sharp instrument, similar to a pencil. Stenciling was also used at San Miguel.

Stenciling Patterns

Activity

Try your hand at stenciling. Paintbrushes were used at the missions, but sponges make stenciling easier.

Directions

1. On heavy paper, draw a design pattern that has parts that can be cut out. For ideas, look at these patterns from Mission San Miguel Arcangel. Cut out the pieces.

2. Place the stencil on top of another piece of paper where the actual stenciled picture will show.

3. Pour a little paint on a paper plate, watered down slightly.

4. Dab the corner of a damp sponge into the paint on the plate.

5. Dab the painted corner of the sponge onto the cut-out areas of the stencil.

6. When all cut-out areas have been painted, carefully lift off the stencil. Let the painted paper dry.

San Antonio de Padua Mission

City: Jolon (Hunter Liggett Military Reservation)
Founded: July 14, 1771
Order of founding: 3rd
Founder: Padre Junipero Serra

San Antonio de Padua is located in the beautiful Valley of the Oaks in the Santa Lucia Mountains. It was the first mission that was not on the coast. It is still very isolated and gives the feel of the area during mission times.

When he first arrived in the valley, Padre Serra rang a bell hung from a tree near the location where the mission would be built. One young Indian man came to watch. He was given gifts of colored beads and fruit. Serra was so kind that the Indian left and returned with other members of his tribe. They brought gifts of acorns, pine nuts, seeds, and rabbits. Serra stayed for two weeks and then left padres Miguel Pieras and Buenaventura Sitjar in charge. The friendly Indians helped build a storehouse, a chapel, and quarters for padres and soldiers.

Soon, an old Indian woman came and asked to be baptized. This surprised the padres—they hadn't been there long enough for her to know what baptisms were! She said that her father had told her a story about a man wearing a robe who had come from the sky four times, telling about Christianity. The story was similar to a well-known Southwest legend, probably from New Mexico. There, in 1620, early missionaries were surprised to find Indians who already knew about the Catholic Church. The story was traced to a nun in Spain who said she had made many visits to the Southwest Indians through supernatural means. Although she never left Spain, her stories accurately described events and places in the Southwest! It is a mystery how the San Antonio Indians would know this legend, although some feel that they may have migrated from New Mexico, because their language was similar.

The first year, the weather was either freezing cold or burning hot. Water sources dried up and crops died. The next year, the missionaries moved the mission near San Miguel Creek. They built a three-mile water channel from the San Antonio River to bring water closer to the fields for crop irrigation. With reliable water, the mission grew abundant wheat crops and raised fine horses. There were also large herds of sheep and cattle. The water system was so well built that ranchers used it years after the mission had been abandoned. In 1806, a water-powered gristmill that ground grain into flour was built. It became famous throughout the mission chain and was the first mill of its kind in California.

An adobe chapel with a tile roof was built in 1782. This is the first known use of the tile roofs in California. They later became a trademark of California and Southwest architecture. A new church was started in 1779 and finished the next year.

On Easter in 1780, the wheat crop was almost destroyed by a heavy frost. The missionaries flooded the field with water to thaw it out. Then they prayed for nine days. Afterward, they had the best crop ever! The padres felt that this showed the Indians the power of their religious faith. San Antonio de Padua grew to become one of the largest missions. The present church was started in 1810 and finished in 1813.

At secularization, the Indians all over California were given the right to vote, but few were actually allowed to. San Antonio de Padua is the only mission known to have held an election that let Indians vote.

After secularization in 1834, a government administrator moved into the mission with his family. Padre Jose Gutierrez was given a back room at the mission. He became paralyzed, received little help, and left in 1844. The Indians were mistreated by the new government and were forced back into the mountains. The Mexican governor, Pio Pico, tried to sell the mission, but nobody bid on it because it was in ruins. When the United States gained control of California in 1846, the mission was returned to the church, but they had no way of maintaining it.

The first attempt at restoration began in 1903 by the California Landmarks Commission, but the work that was started was destroyed by the earthquake of 1906. Work continued very slowly and restoration of the church was finished in 1907. Current restoration started in 1948 with a $50,000 grant from the William Randolph Hearst Foundation. Except for the church, the buildings were stripped to the ground and rebuilt as a replica of the 1813 mission. Old materials and methods were used whenever possible, but the buildings were strengthened with steel and concrete. The main altar has four original statues. That had been saved by the Indians and stored during years when the mission was deserted. Restoration continues today.

San Antonio de Padua is the only mission located on a military reservation. It shares land with the Hunter Liggett Military Reservation. It is a well-known area for spring wildflowers, particularly poppies and lupine.

Creating a Dictionary

One reason for the success of Mission San Antonio de Padua was Padre Sitjar. He was an excellent leader, and the Indians loved him. He worked at the mission for 37 years, except for a short break in the late 1790s when he helped establish nearby Mission San Miguel. Sitjar was able to teach the Indians Christianity because he learned the Mutsun language spoken by the locals. He was the first to write down the vocabulary and grammar of their language. His 400-page book is now preserved at the Smithsonian Institution in Washington, DC. Padre Sitjar found his Mutsun dictionary helpful in understanding words that were new to him.

Dictionaries tell many things about a word, including

- spelling—how to spell the word

- capital letters—whether or not the word needs to be capitalized

- syllable division—where to divide the word and place the hyphen(s)

- accent marks—which syllable(s) should be stressed when saying the word

- pronunciation—how to say the word, showing phonetic spelling

- parts of speech—the part of speech of the word, such as *noun* or *verb*

- word history—where the word came from or how the meaning has changed over time

- synonyms and antonyms—words with similar or opposite meanings

- meaning—the word may have one or more definitions

- illustration—a picture of the word may be shown

Activity

Write your own dictionary for words that deal with California missions. Include as many of the ten items listed to the left as possible. You might also want to include guide words at the top of your pages and pronunciation keys at the bottom of the pages. Look closely at a real dictionary page to learn the layout elements of a page, such as alphabetizing and the arrangement of word entries. You can write this dictionary by yourself or as a group project.

You should include the following words, but you can certainly add more: *adobe, alcalde, asistencia, atole, carreta, governor, lavanderia, mayordomo, mission, missionary, neophyte, padre, presidio, pueblo, quadrangle, restoration, secularization, tallow, tanner, viceroy.*

Nuestra Señora de la Soledad Mission

City: Soledad
Founded: October 9, 1791
Order of founding: 13th
Founder: Padre Fermin de Lasuen

Padre de Lasuen founded Nuestra Señora de la Soledad in the Salinas Valley. It was a long walking distance between Missions San Antonio de Padua and San Carlos Borromeo del Rio Carmelo, so the new mission at Soledad provided a rest stop. The buildings went up slowly. A temporary church was built in about a year, but it took six years before a large church was built. This thatched-roof adobe church was completed in 1797 and enlarged in 1805.

In the early years, the mission did well, although it was in an area without many Indians and didn't have large numbers of religious converts. An epidemic also killed many Indians; others were afraid of the disease and left. Nuestra Señora de la Soledad ranked in the middle of all the missions in terms of agricultural production. There were large herds of cattle, sheep, and horses. During the dry summer months, irrigation water was piped from the Salinas River, so crops could grow in the hot Salinas Valley. Some years there were droughts without enough rainfall for the crops, and in other years too much rain fell. Several times, floods ruined crops and buildings.

Because life was so difficult at Nuestra Señora de la Soledad, and the mission so isolated, padres did not stay long. Many asked to be reassigned after only one year. Almost 30 padres served at Soledad in its 44-year existence. The rooms were very hot in the summer and cold, gloomy, and damp in the winter. Many padres suffered from rheumatism and lung diseases due to the cold winters.

Padre Florencio Ibanez was a gentle man and was good to the Indians. He loved and respected them and taught them to read and write. Ibanez also taught them music and often wrote plays for them. He spent 15 years at Nuestra Senora de la Soledad, the longest of any padre. He stayed the longest only because there was no one to replace him. He died at age 78 in 1818 and is buried at Soledad. One of Padre Ibanez's friends, Jose Joaquin de Arrillaga, first Spanish governor of Alta California, died at Soledad while touring the missions in 1814. He was buried beneath the church floor. The graves were destroyed by flooding.

Padre Vicente Francisco de Sarria served as padre from 1828 until he died in 1835. He also loved the Indians. The College of San Fernando could send him no more missionaries, so he kept the mission going himself. The mission became so poor that the crops could not feed everyone. Sarria often gave his share of the food to the Indians. On a Sunday morning in May, he collapsed at the altar from starvation and died that afternoon. The few remaining Indians carried his body on a litter 25 miles to Mission San Antonio de Padua for burial. With their kind padre gone, the Indians did not want to stay. The mission fell into disrepair. The roof tiles were taken off and sold to the Mexican government to pay debts. With the tiles gone, the adobe walls were unprotected and decayed into ruins.

Feliciano Soberanes was asked by Governor Alvarado in 1841 to take charge of the 8,900 acres belonging to Mission Soledad. The governor was replaced by General Micheltorena, who stopped at the mission and demanded 40 horses, 50 head of cattle, four yoke of oxen, and some sheep. Soberanes had no choice. He demanded payment of $800, but it was refused. Then Soberanes petitioned the Mexican government and said the $800 debt could be cancelled if he was granted Mission Soledad and its lands. The petition was granted, and the Soberanes family continued to accumulate land; eventually they became the largest land owners in Monterey County.

After the United States took over California, the mission was returned to the Catholic Church in 1859. Nothing was done to protect and care for the buildings for years. Only one corner of the walls remained intact, plus several mounds of adobe, when the Native Daughters of the Golden West restored the chapel and padres' wing in the 1950s and 1960s.

Naming the Missions

Mission life was difficult at Nuestra Señora de la Soledad because this inland mission was so isolated. Its name even reflects this isolation! In 1769, many years before Nuestra Señora de la Soledad was founded, Captain Gaspar de Portola and Padre Juan Crespi camped in the area where Mission Nuestra Señora de la Soledad would later be founded. They were traveling north up the Salinas Valley looking for the port of Monterey. They met a Costanoan Indian, who kept repeating *soledad*. It apparently was the name they called themselves, but it sounded like the Spanish word for loneliness. It was an appropriate name for this lonely, isolated mission. Two years later when Padre Serra stopped here, returning to Carmel after founding San Antonio de Padua, he talked briefly with the Indians. When he asked an Indian woman her name, her answer also sounded like *soledad*. In 1849, a visitor wrote: "A more desolate place cannot well be imagined." When Hippolyte de Bouchard, the pirate, raided the coastal missions in 1818, many of the religious and governmental leaders from the coast hid at isolated Nuestra Señora de la Soledad.

The missions were often named for Catholic saints. A saint is a person officially recognized as having lived an exceptionally holy life. Saints are appointed by a commission of the Catholic Church, which examines the person's life. If there is enough evidence, the person is eligible for beatification, which means that he or she may officially be declared "blessed." If further investigation finds proof of two miracles associated with the person, he or she may be canonized as a saint. Only the pope can officially name a saint.

Activity

Name the mission whose name origin is being described:

Origin of the Mission's Name

Mission Name

1. **Saint John of Capistrano (1385–1456)**—He studied law and was a governor in Italy. He organized a crusade against the Turks.

   1. _____

2. **Saint Louis, Bishop of Toulouse (1274–1297)**—With his two younger brothers, he was held hostage in Barcelona, Spain for seven years in exchange for their father, the king of Naples, who was captured in a naval battle. During this time, he was taught by Franciscan friars and was later the bishop of Toulouse (France).

   2. _____

Naming the Missions (continued)

Origin of the Mission's Name   **Mission Name**

3. **Saint Didacus (about 1400–1463)**—He was a Franciscan missionary to the Canary Islands, a miraculous healer in Rome, and the head of an infirmary in Spain. The mission was also named for a nearby bay that had been named 167 years earlier by the Spanish explorer Sebastian Vizcaino. The custom was for explorers to name sites in honor of the saint whose feast day was near.

3. _____

4. **Saint Claire of Assisi (1194–1253)**—She was the founder of the order of nuns called the Poor Clares. This order was based on the Franciscans. It was the first mission to honor a woman in its name.

4. _____

5. **"The Most Pure (Immaculate) Conception of Mary Most Holy," the mother of Jesus.**—Her conception of Jesus is called the Immaculate Conception.

5. _____

6. **Saint Agnes**—She was a 13-year-old Roman girl killed in 304 A.D. for refusing to make a pagan sacrifice and believing in Christ during the persecutions of the Christians by Emperor Diocletian.

6. _____

7. **Saint Barbara**—According to legend, she was the beautiful daughter of Dioscorus of Nicomedia, a pagan Roman ruler. Her father became so angry when she became a Christian that he imprisoned her in a tower and finally cut off her head with his own sword. Her father was immediately struck dead by a bolt of lightning.

7. _____

8. **Saint Raphael**—He was one of the archangels named in the Bible. His name means "God heals," and he is the patron saint of travelers, joy, and good health.

8. _____

9. **Saint Bonaventure (1221–1274)**—He was born Giovanni de Fidanza in Italy. The name _Bonaventure_ was given to him by St. Francis when he healed a four-year-old boy and exclaimed, "O! Buona ventura!" (which means "good fortune"). He was a great scholar and writer and worked to unify the Eastern and Western churches.

9. _____

10. **King Ferdinand III of Spain (1198–1252)**—He was successful in driving the Moors out of most of Spain and started churches in those areas.

10. _____

11. **Gabriel, God's Messenger Angel**—He is one of the archangels mentioned in the Bible. He is mentioned twice in the Book of Daniel—announcing the birth of John the Baptist and the coming of Jesus.

11. _____

Naming the Missions (continued)

Origin of the Mission's Name

Mission Name

12. **Saint John the Baptist (about 7 B.C.–28 A.D.)**—He was a prophet who predicted the coming of the Messiah (Jesus) and who baptized Jesus.

12. _____

13. **Saint Francis Solano (Solanus)**—He was born in Spain in 1549 of noble parents. He was a missionary among the Indians of Peru. He had a remarkable ability to learn Native American languages.

13. _____

14. **King Louis IX (1214–1270)**—He became king of France at age 12 when his father died. He was considered an ideal ruler. Even his enemies admired his fairness. He led two crusades, or holy wars. The first was to Egypt, where he was taken captive. The second was to Tunis, where he died of typhus. He was named a saint of his crusades.

14. _____

15. **Saint Michael**—He is considered the chief archangel and protector of Christians, particularly at the time of death. He is the leader of God's Army against Satan.

15. _____

16. **Saint Joseph**—He was the husband of Mary, who was the mother of Jesus. He was a carpenter in Nazareth.

16. _____

17. **Saint Anthony, Patron of the Poor (1195–1231)**—People pray to this famous preacher for the return of lost articles. He was a brilliant scholar.

17. _____

18. **Our Most Sorrowful Lady of Solitude**—This name tells of the sorrow that Mary, the mother of Jesus, felt after he had been crucified.

18. _____

19. **Saint Charles Borromeo (1538–1584)**—He was an Italian and the first great leader of the Counter-Reformation. He played an important part in church government.

19. _____

20. **Holy Cross (Sacred Cross)**—The cross on which Christ died is a symbol of Christianity.

20. _____

21. **Saint Francis of Assisi (1182–1226)**—He was born into a wealthy Italian family, but gave it up for a simple life of poverty, which was an inspiration to others. He founded the Franciscan Order. He was known for his love of peace and also his respect for all living creatures.

21. _____

San Carlos Borromeo del Rio Carmelo Mission

City: Carmel
Founded: June 3, 1770
Order of founding: 2nd
Founder: Padre Junipero Serra

Monterey was intended to be the site of Spain's most northern mission. It was hoped that this mission would slow the Russians from moving further south down the Pacific Coast. The Monterey mission's location was chosen based on the glowing description of Monterey Bay by the Spanish explorer, Sebastian Vizcaino, in 1602. Years later in 1769, Gaspar de Portola had searched for the bay but thought he hadn't found the correct bay. He planted a cross near the bay he had found and continued his search. Portola and his men returned the next year and realized they had found Monterey Bay the year before after all! The cross was still there, now surrounded by arrows, feathers, and fish left by the Indians. The Indians later told the Spaniards strange tales of the cross—how it mysteriously glowed at night and, at times, grew tall enough to reach the sky. The Indians had brought offerings to the cross.

In 1770, a week after Portola arrived by land, Padre Serra arrived by sea. Padre Serra founded the second mission near the beach, while Portola claimed the land for Spain and founded the new presidio where Spanish soldiers would be stationed to protect the mission. It is said that when the news of the mission's founding reached Mexico City, the bells of its churches rang out in joy. Portola turned his command over to Lieutenant Pedro Fages and returned to Mexico. Serra and the soldiers built brush shelters for barracks, warehouses, and a chapel.

Within a year, Serra moved the mission five miles south to the more fertile Carmel Valley,

beside a stream. The site was described as "two gunshots" (2,400–2,800 feet; 731.5–853.5 meters) from the ocean. The new site had more Indians and was further away from the bad influence of the soldiers. Today, the mission is often called the Carmel Mission because of its location in Carmel, California.

The present building is the seventh to stand on the site. This sandstone church was started in 1793 under the direction of Padre Lasuen. He brought a master stonemason, Manuel Ruiz, from Mexico to design and build the church. It was completed in 1797. Some say that the unique star window was originally intended to have been placed on its side as a rectangle.

The mission did well, though there were troubles over the years. It had a small Indian population. The Esselen Indians who lived near the mission were friendly. In 1803, an epidemic of influenza killed at least 86 Indians, and many others fled into the hills. In 1814, the vaulted stone roof had to be replaced due to earthquake damage. In 1818, Hippolyte de Bouchard, the pirate, attacked the presidio at Monterey. For six days he plundered Monterey, burning buildings, robbing stores, capturing livestock, and destroying orchards. It was feared that the pirate would attack the mission as well. After hiding the mission's treasures, the padres escaped to Mission Nuestra Señora de la Soledad to hide. When they returned, they found the mission had not been touched.

Serra made San Carlos Borromeo del Rio Carmelo the capital of all the California missions. This mission became a favorite, and until 1803, other mission presidents used it as their headquarters, too. Serra stayed at Carmel when he was not founding and caring for his eight other missions. He took his vows of poverty seriously. He lived in a tiny room where his only belongings were a board cot, blanket, table, chair, chest, candlestick, and gourd. Serra suffered from a tubercular infection and, at age 71, knew he was dying. He asked his lifelong friend, Padre Palou, to prepare him for death. He died at Carmel on August 28, 1784 and, at his request, was buried in the church sanctuary beside Padre Juan Crespi, his dear friend. Padres Lopez and Lasuen were also buried in the sanctuary.

After secularization in 1834, San Carlos Borromeo del Rio Carmelo suffered from neglect. The Mexican governor, Pio Pico, tried to sell the mission in 1846, but there was little left of value. In 1852, the roof timbers collapsed under the weight of the roof tiles. For 30 years the church had no cover. The land was sold right up to the mission door. Sand drifted in, covering the floor, so grasses and weeds grew tall. A visitor in 1861 wrote: ". . . hundreds (literally) of squirrels scampered around their holes in the old walls; cattle had free access to all parts; and thousands of birds, apparently, lived in nooks in the old deserted walls."

In 1882, Father Angelo Casanova opened the tombs in the sanctuary to over 400 viewers. By showing Serra's remains, he stopped a rumor that they had been removed. This viewing focused attention on the mission.

In 1884, Casanova was able to collect money for its restoration. A steep-pitched shingle roof was added to protect the walls. It didn't match the architectural style and was criticized until its removal in 1934, when an accurate tile restoration was done. The chapel was rededicated in 1884, in time to celebrate the 100-year anniversary of Serra's death. In 1960, Pope John XXIII made Mission San Carlos Borromeo del Rio Carmelo a minor basilica, which gave it certain ceremonial privileges. It is now one of the most beautiful missions.

Mission Libraries

Mission San Carlos Borromeo del Rio Carmelo had the first library in the state of California. Mission libraries were important in the daily lives of the people. The books provided information on theology, agriculture, history, geography, architecture, and medicine. The collection of books at this mission came from several sources:

- Mexico City's San Fernando Apostolic College

- Mexican missions

- Baja California missions

Each book was numbered at the top of the spine, telling the bookcase number and the shelf position.

In 1778, the library had a collection of about 30 books which had grown to 302 books when it was first catalogued in 1800 by Padre Lasuen. At secularization, the inventory listed 179 titles from 404 individual books. When the mission was abandoned, the books were dispersed, mostly around Monterey. In 1949, 229 of the original books of the 1770–1842 library were returned. The library now has approximately 600 books. Today, visitors to the mission can see the re-created library.

Activity

Imagine that your school or public library has no books on the California missions. Your job is to write a recommended list of at least three books that you think would be important for the library to buy. Write the following information about each book:

1. Write the following in proper bibliography format. List the books alphabetically, according to the author's last name. There are several variations of bibliography formats, but here is one example:

Smith, Chris. *California Mission Music*. San Francisco, CA: History Books of America Publishing Company, 1995.

Author

Title

City and state where it was published

Publishing company name

Year it was published

2. From a library, find out the call number (shelf location number) of the book.

3. Write a paragraph telling what information the book includes and why the library should purchase the book.

San Juan Bautista Mission

City: San Juan Bautista
Founded: June 24, 1797
Order of founding: 15th
Founder: Padre Fermin de Lasuen

Padre de Lasuen selected the site for Mission San Juan Bautista in a beautiful valley filled with oak trees. The mission was a success from the beginning. Construction began almost immediately under the supervision of Padres Jose Martiarena and Pedro Martinez. The Indians were friendly and helped the missionaries build an adobe church and other mission buildings within six months.

By the late 1790s, there were over 500 Indians living at the mission. The church was soon too small for the many neophytes who came to the church. The padres couldn't decide if they should make the old church larger or build a new church. In 1798, when 20 days of earthquakes damaged the church between October 11 and 31, they had to rebuild, but they also made it larger.

An even larger church was soon needed as more Indians came to the mission. In June 1803, the governor and other dignitaries were invited to the laying of the cornerstone of the present church. A bottle containing the story of the dedication was placed into the cornerstone and is still there today.

In 1808, a new padre, Felipe del Arroyo de la Cuesta, arrived. He expected the Indian population to continue to grow and decided that the new church should be able to hold 1,000 people. The architectural plans were changed, and when the church was finished, it was the largest and only church of its kind with three aisles, side-by-side. The church was dedicated on June 23, 1812.

Unfortunately, the Indian population began to decline. Many Indians died of disease and others left. Two of the aisles were closed off because of the decline and were used to gain more solid construction due to frequent earthquakes. Wild animal tracks can be found on the church tiles inside the church! During mission days, newly formed tiles were set out in the field to dry. At night, deer, bobcats, bears, and other animals walked over them while they were still soft.

San Juan Bautista had some padres who were strong leaders. Padre Estevan Tapis retired as president of the California missions and came to San Juan Bautista in 1812. His musical talents gave a new name to the mission, the "Mission of Music." Indians were attracted to the mission because of his music and the Indian boys' choir. Tapis used colored notes to identify the different vocal parts. He colored notes in red, white, black, and yellow. Each person learned his or her part by following the appropriate color.

Padre Cuesta was a great scholar. He was interested in Indian ways of life and their languages. Cuesta was able to give his sermons in seven San Juan Indian dialects. In later years, when rheumatism stiffened his bones and confined him to a chair, he wrote a study of the Mutsun Indian language. Cuesta was also an architect and musician. He was a gentle man and especially fond of children. Since he was a classical scholar, he loved to give the Indians Christian names of famous people, such as Alexander, Plato, and Cicero.

From time to time there were troubles with the Tulare Indians. One night in 1798, Indians surrounded the mission but were persuaded to leave peaceably. The next year, an Indian raid resulted in the death of eight neophytes. Spanish soldiers reacted severely, which brought an uneasy peace for a while. Indian raids stopped the longest when, during an attack, the Indians were entranced and calmed by the music of the mission's barrel organ. They not only declared peace for several years, but many stayed and joined the mission so that they could hear the organ regularly.

Secularization occurred in 1835. Much of the mission property was taken by the Mexican government. In 1859, after California joined the United States, the mission buildings and 55 acres were returned to the church by federal decree. San Juan Bautista has always had a priest in residence, so it was never damaged by vandals or neglect. Several architectural changes occurred over the years, but the original style was restored in 1949.

Restoration work started on the mission in 1884. The mission walls collapsed in the great earthquake of 1906 that nearly destroyed San Francisco. It was rebuilt in 1975–1976 with steel, reinforced concrete, and heavy cross-bracing. Below the cemetery wall is a rare original stretch of the El Camino Real, the north-south road that joined the missions. San Juan Bautista was a bit east of the original road, but a loop was added to include the mission.

Today, visitors can get an idea of what the San Juan Bautista community looked like in the 1800s. Around the plaza is a hotel, stable, and two adobe houses. These original buildings were restored and the plaza area is now operated as a State Historic Park.

Earthquake Model

Mission San Juan Bautista might just as well have been named for Saint Andrew, because it was built in the San Benito Valley directly over the San Andreas Fault. This is the longest and most active earthquake fault in California. It runs along the base of the hill below the mission's cemetery wall. Over the years, many earthquakes have struck this area. In 1906, the side walls of the church collapsed.

Activity

Make a model of an earthquake with a dessert gelatin by following these instructions:

Materials

- Two 6-oz. (170-g) boxes of purple or red (closest to soil color) dessert gelatin
- Two one-serving envelopes of unflavored gelatin
- 4 cups (1 L) boiling water
- 4 cups (1 L) cold water
- 9" x 12" (22.75 cm x 30.5 cm) metal baking pan
- Plastic wrap
- Sugar cubes

Directions

1. Empty the dessert gelatin and the unflavored gelatin into the metal baking pan. Add boiling water and stir until the powder is dissolved. Add the cold water and stir. The mixture should fill the pan nearly to the top. Chill at least three hours or until set.

2. *Review this information:* Under the soil are rock layers. These layers are under stress because of the activity within the earth. When the layers are under stress, they react like silicone putty (Silly Putty™), which will snap into two pieces when given a sharp tug. Energy is released in the form of waves.

3. Use the gelatin to show this energy release. Holding the pan firmly, gently tap its side. Watch the waves travel through the gelatin. The gelatin is like the ground, the tap of the hand is like the rock breaking, and the waves in the gelatin are like earthquake waves. Predict what will happen when the pan is tapped harder.

4. Cover the top of the gelatin with plastic wrap so it will be clean enough to eat later. Be sure that the wrap touches the gelatin. To find out what happens to buildings during an earthquake, build sugar-cube or domino "buildings" on top of the gelatin. Tap on the side of the pan. Did the buildings fall over? Rebuild the buildings so that they are more resistant to an "earthquake."

5. Enjoy eating your gelatin!

Santa Cruz Mission

City: Santa Cruz
Founded: September 25, 1791
Order of founding: 12th
Founder: Padre Fermin de Lasuen

Early travelers were impressed with the Santa Cruz area. When Captain Gaspar de Portola's group of explorers passed through the area in 1769, they were amazed at the giant redwood trees. In 1776, Padre Palou reported on Santa Cruz's good location. As a result of these reports, Padre de Lasuen founded Mission Santa Cruz at a site on the north end of Monterey Bay. It had a good climate, fertile soil, fresh water, and friendly Indians. The area was rich in game, grasses, and berries. Temporary buildings were made from split redwood, but the rainy season showed that the mission was too close to the water, so it was moved to higher ground overlooking the San Lorenzo River and Pacific Ocean. The church was started February 27, 1793 and dedicated May 10, 1794. The quadrangle and gristmill were soon finished.

The mission had a promising beginning. Unfortunately, it struggled through difficult times. The total population of Mission Santa Cruz was the lowest of any mission. The mission's biggest problem was the building of a pueblo across the river. Spanish law forbade pueblos from being built near missions. Missionaries were against having presidios and pueblos too close to missions because of the bad influence on the Indians. This third pueblo in California was allowed, however, despite protests of the padres. The mission was expected to support the pueblo, named Branciforte in honor of the viceroy, the Spanish king's representative in Mexico. The town was to be a planned, model community by the private developer, Diego de Borica. He used a promotional scheme to attract settlers but, despite promises, no houses had been built for them.

The padres' worst fears were realized when settlers arrived from San Blas, Mexico in July 1797. Instead of good citizens, nine gamblers and thieves arrived with their families. These 17 people were sick, poor, lazy, and immoral. The men had been given the choice of going to jail or settling in Santa Cruz. In order to get more settlers to California, they were offered land and money to settle there. More of the same undesirable characters arrived later. The settlers took over some mission lands and mistreated the Indians. When the padres complained, the governor defended the settlers, saying that the Indians were dying out anyway and soon there would be no need for the mission!

The padres had to take strict measures to protect the Indians from the people of Branciforte. It was probably a result of these restraints that caused the death of Padre Andres Quintana. He was found dead in bed. It was thought that he died from natural causes, but two years later there were suspicions that he had actually been killed. The first autopsy in California's history was performed. Seven neophytes were charged with murder. In their defense, they pleaded that they had been treated with excessive cruelty by the padre. The governor could find no evidence to support this, so the Indians were given severe floggings.

In 1798, rain and high winds damaged mission buildings. The next year, floods did more damage. The buildings had to be repaired. More difficulties hit in 1818 when the pirate,

Hyppolite de Bouchard, arrived along the California coast. He had attacked the Monterey Presidio and it was feared that he would also attack Mission Santa Cruz. Governor Pablo de Sola ordered Padre Ramon Olbes to have the people of Branciforte pack the mission valuables and send them inland. Olbes and the neophytes escaped to Mission Nuestra Señora de la Soledad for safety.

Bouchard did not land at Santa Cruz, but he probably couldn't have done more damage than what occurred instead. The people of Branciforte carried out the order but helped themselves to the mission's food and drank most of the wine and brandy. These drunk settlers looted the mission. When Olbes returned, he found the mission almost ruined. Valuables had been stolen and the inside of the church was damaged. The settlers didn't return the things that they were suppose to save. Olbes was so angry and upset that he asked to leave the mission, but the request was denied.

As Branciforte grew, the mission declined. Branciforte became a haven for smugglers. Mission Santa Cruz was one of the first missions to be secularized. The land was granted to settlers and the Indians left.

The church tower fell in 1840 and the buildings gradually decayed and collapsed. By 1846, there was little left for the Mexican governor, Pio Pico, to sell. The church collapsed in 1857 a month after two severe earthquakes. The crash was so loud that it awakened the village at 3 A.M. A frame church replaced the adobe church in 1858 and stood until 1889, when it was replaced by the church now standing on the town square.

In 1931, a small replica of the mission church was built near the original site and was donated to the church. The facade design of the replica was based on early sketches. The inside was not copied from the original, but it contains items from the mission such as statues, candlesticks, and paintings. Today, the mission replica is used for weddings and private masses. Branciforte is the east side of Santa Cruz.

Constructing a Sundial

The people at the California missions told time by using sundials, or shadow clocks. As the sun moves from east to west during the day, the shadows that it casts move, too. A sundial tells time by measuring the angle of the shadows cast by the sun. The Babylonians learned to tell time this way over 4,000 years ago.

There are many types of sundials, but they all work on the same principle. Every sundial has an upright called a gnomon (NO-mon). The base has a series of lines on it and each one is marked in hours. When sunlight hits the gnomon, it casts a shadow onto the base. The shadow will fall on or between different lines and mark the time of day. Sundials measure local time.

Activity

Construct a sundial made from a flowerpot and a stick. The stick forms the gnomon, and the base of the pot is the dial.

Materials

- Flowerpot
- Stick (twice the height of the flowerpot)
- Black marker

Directions

1. In a sunny location, turn the flowerpot upside down and place it on the ground.

2. Push the stick through the hole in the bottom of flowerpot and into the ground.

3. Mark the position that the stick's shadow casts exactly every hour. With the black marker, label the mark, telling what time it is. For example, at 10:00 A.M., trace the shadow line and label it *10:00 A.M.*

4. Go outside the next day and use the sundial clock to tell the time.

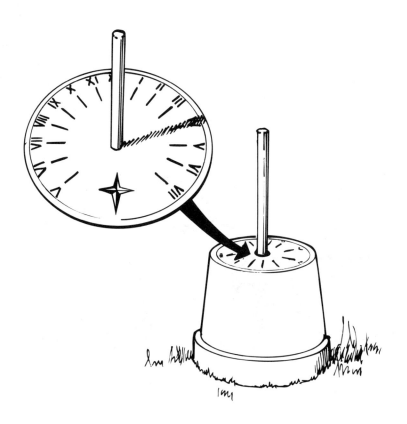

74

Santa Clara de Asis Mission

City: Santa Clara
Founded: January 12, 1777
Order of founding: 8th
Founder: Padre Junipero Serra

Santa Clara de Asis was built to protect San Francisco Bay. The governor sent Lieutenant Jose Joaquin Moraga and Padre Tomas de la Pena, with soldiers and their families, to start this new mission. They chose a site at the south end of San Francisco Bay. A few weeks later they were joined by Padre Jose Antonio Murguia from Monterey, who brought church supplies, livestock, and tools.

The Indians in the area were numerous and friendly; however, they stole some of the Spaniards' mules for food. Soldiers from the presidio in San Francisco found the Indians in their village, eating the mule meat. A battle took place, killing three Indians. Some of the Indian leaders were captured and taken to the mission to be flogged. In May, an epidemic struck and many Indian children died. Indian parents brought about 50 children to be baptized, hoping to save them from death.

In November, a few months after the mission was founded, settlers were brought to the area by Lieutenant Moraga. They built the pueblo of San Jose across the river from the mission. This was the first civil (non-mission) Spanish town in California. There were serious tensions between the people of Santa Clara de Asis and the town of San Jose. There were disputes over property lines, the mingling of settlers' cattle with mission herds, and Guadalupe River water rights. Padre Magin Catala helped lessen the tension by uniting the two groups with a road. With the help of soldiers and Indians, they built a four-mile "Alameda" between the mission and the town. To make the road more pleasant, it was lined with black willow trees. On Sundays, churchgoers dressed in their best silk and satin clothes took horse-drawn carriages or fine horses down this unpaved avenue between the church and town.

The mission was rebuilt several times during its history due to floods, fires, and earthquakes. The original wooden mission was destroyed by a flood on January 23, 1779. Padre Serra blessed a second, temporary wood church on November 11, 1779. On November 19, 1781, Padre Serra laid the cornerstone to start a permanent adobe church. In the cornerstone he placed a cross, other religious objects, and Spanish coins to signify the church treasury. These long-forgotten items were later dug up in 1911 by a crew laying a gas main. The new church was dedicated by Padre Serra on May 15, 1784, but Padre Murguia, who had worked so hard on its design and built it along with the Indians, had died four days earlier. This new church was the most elaborate building in California at the time.

One of the reasons why the mission was so successful was that Padres Jose Viader and Magin Catala served the mission from the 1790s to the 1830s. Viader used his musical talent to train an excellent choir of Indians. He was a tall, muscular man with a big heart. However, one night three Indians attacked him. The padre was so strong that he soundly thrashed all three. He forgave them and gave them a severe lecture on their conduct. The padre's behavior so impressed the Indians' leader, Marcelo, that he became a Catholic convert and close friend of the padre.

Padre Catala also lived at the mission for many years. He was dearly loved by the Indians. Besides building the Alameda, he was known for being a prophet. The Indians believed that he could tell the future—Catala predicted that Spain would no longer rule the land, that gold would be found in California, and that San Francisco would be damaged by an earthquake and fire—all of which took place.

In 1812, an earthquake damaged Santa Clara de Asis. It was still being repaired in 1818 when another earthquake convinced the padres to move the mission again. The fifth and present site was chosen. A temporary adobe church was constructed and used until the permanent one was dedicated on August 11, 1825. This building, with various modifications, stood until 1926.

Despite the difficulty of establishing church buildings, the mission became one of the most successful. The mission was blessed with competent padres, a good climate, and rich soil. The church was known for its abundant crops of peaches, pears, figs, grapes, and grain, plus a large herd of cattle.

After secularization, Santa Clara de Asis continued as a church even though its wealth and possessions were gone. In 1850, Father John Nobili was able to get back some of the mission land to start a school. In 1851, a school was approved to help provide more English-speaking church leaders for the new Americans. Classes began in May of 1855 at Santa Clara College.

Renovation of the crumbling mission church began in 1861. In 1885, adobe walls were replaced with wood framing, and the interior was widened. In the spring, old adobes stacked on the ground sprouted wildflowers in the spring from seeds that had been sealed in the adobe walls for 60 years!

In 1926, a fire began in a bell tower of the remodeled church, caused by faulty wiring that had been eroded by bat guano! A priest saying morning mass gave the alarm. Students and faculty tried to save the historic building. The church was destroyed, but many of the artifacts were rescued. The present church, dedicated October 12, 1929, is a replica of the 1825 church before its many remodelings.

The school that Nobili started is now the University of Santa Clara. It became a university in 1912, and is the oldest in California. Santa Clara de Asis is located near the entrance of the university and is the only mission to become part of a university. It serves as a parish church and a college chapel. The beautiful mission gardens are part of the university campus. This garden has more of its original plants than any other surviving mission garden.

Cardboard Loom Weaving

The purpose of the missions was not only to convert Indians to Christianity, but also to change them into a useful working class for the new Spanish colony. Neophytes were taught European home and farm skills. Skilled craftsmen were always needed during mission times in California. They were often specially recruited from Mexico, paid by government contract, and expected to train Indian neophytes in their particular craft.

Women were taught to spin and weave. The blankets and cloth that they produced in the mission workshops were used in the presidios, missions, and pueblos. Santa Clara de Asis was famous for its fine weaving.

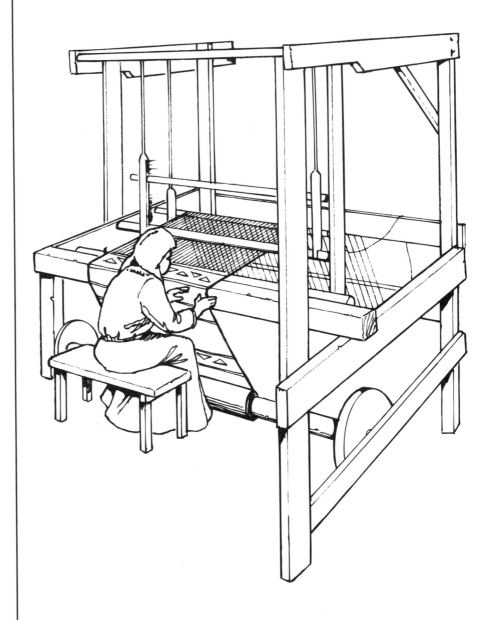

Cardboard Loom Weaving

Activity

Large looms were used at the missions, but weaving can also be done on small cardboard looms.

Materials

- 9" x 12" (22.75 cm x 30.5 cm) cardboard
- Ruler or pencil
- Thin, strong string
- Scissors
- Yarn of any weight or color

Directions

1. Measure and mark a ½-inch (1.25-cm) border on each nine-inch (22.75-cm) edge of the cardboard. Draw a mark every ½ inch (1.25 cm). Cut slits on the ½-inch (1.25-cm) marks that are ½ inch (1.25 cm) deep.

2. Tie a knot in one end of the string and slide it under the first ½-inch (1.25-cm) slit. Bring the string across the loom and slide it through the slit directly across. Loop the string under and slip it up through the slit next to it. Continue looping the string to the last slit and knot the end of the string.

3. Weave yarn in and out across the width of the loom. Ribbon and strips of fabric can also be added. Try making designs. Do not pull the yarn tightly, or the weaving will not have a rectangular shape.

4. To finish the weaving, cut the first two loops of string from one end. Tie these two strings together in a knot. Continue to cut and tie all pairs of string. This will remove the weaving from the loom so it can be used again.

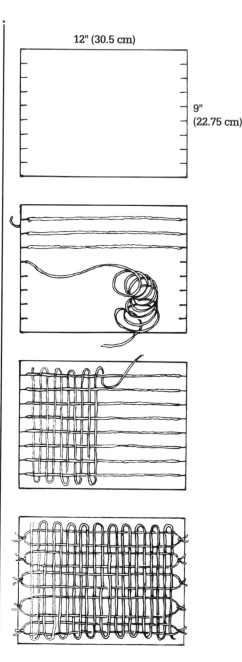

12" (30.5 cm)

9" (22.75 cm)

San Jose Mission

City: Fremont
Founded: June 11, 1797
Order of founding: 14th
Founder: Padre Fermin de Lasuen

Padre de Lasuen wanted new missions built so that they would be located no more than one day apart. This would make for safer travel since the Indians rarely attacked during the day. When permission was granted, a site was found northeast of Santa Clara on the east side of San Francisco Bay. They set up a cross near Alameda Creek, but it took two years to get permission to build the mission. (Note: The Mexican governor chose the name *Mission San Jose*. The name is not *San Jose de Guadalupe*. In the early 1900s, a sign on the roof of the museum had the incorrect name, which is still found in some books.)

Padre de Lasuen dedicated the site and celebrated mass on June 11, 1797. Sergeant Pedro Amador directed the construction of thatched-roof shelters. Cattle, sheep, and other animals were sent from Missions Santa Clara and Dolores. A fiesta was held to honor the beginning of the new mission. The site was near Mill Creek, north of today's mission.

The first year, only 33 Ohlone Indians were converted to Christianity, but the padres kept trying, and San Jose eventually became one of the most successful missions in northern California. A large adobe church in a simple architectural style was completed in 1809 to care for the many converts.

Mission San Jose was involved in an international event. On April 8, 1806, a Russian count, Nikolai Rezanof, sailed into San Francisco Bay aboard his tiny ship, *Juno*. He was looking for supplies for the starving Russian colonists in Sitka, Alaska. The padres gave them corn, flour, and beef in trade for cloth and then put on a fiesta.

Much of the mission's success was due to two capable padres, Buenaventura Fortuni and Narciso Duran. They worked together until Fortuni was transferred to Sonoma. Duran directed the mission for 27 years, was padre-presidente of the mission chain for three terms, constructed irrigation systems, excelled in music, and was an expert planner of military strategies.

More than any other mission, San Jose was a base for military expeditions to control the Indians of the San Joaquin and Sacramento Valleys. Many of these inland Indians were either indifferent or openly hostile to the mission. Runaway neophytes from Mission Dolores were often hidden near San Jose by local Indians. Over the years, there were many raids and skirmishes. For example, in 1805, an Indian asked Padre Pedro de la Cueva to come inland to care for sick Indians. A group of soldiers and a few mission Indians went with the padre. On the way, they were attacked by hostile Indians and many were killed. Cueva escaped into a thick fog.

In 1828, Duran was sad when one of his favorite Indian helpers, Estanislao, defected to the warring tribes. He was bored by the restrictions of mission life and led attacks against settlers in the San Joaquin Valley. He was finally captured by General Mariano Vallejo. Many Indians were killed, but Duran protested the brutality. He later forgave Estanislao, who returned to the mission. He died of smallpox ten years later. Stanislaus County was named for him. In 1883, Duran moved his headquarters to Santa Barbara.

After secularization, the mission declined. All but the church and graveyard were sold for $12,000 by the Mexican governor, Pio Pico. The sale was invalidated when the Americans took over California the next year. Over the years, the buildings had different uses. A store was operated at the mission during the Gold Rush, and it became a busy center for supplying the southern mines. The mission was also used as a saloon and hotel in the 1860s. The buildings had been slowly deteriorating when the mission was destroyed in a violent earthquake in 1868.

After the earthquake, a wooden church was built directly over the original foundations, and later, a rectory was built on the grounds. To make room for the reconstruction of the church, these buildings were moved to other locations. By 1985, the reconstruction was complete. It was modeled after the mission in the 1830s and was built on the original foundations. Original tools, styles, and materials were used to give an authentic look. Today, the mission is located in Fremont, 13 miles from the city of San Jose. Mission Santa Clara is actually closer to the city of San Jose than Mission San Jose is.

80

Mission Music

usic was an important part of mission life. Both the Indians and the Spanish used chants and songs in their worship and during work. The religious music attracted the Indians to the missions. Through music, the padres were able to teach the Indians about Christianity.

Padre Narciso Duran excelled in music, although he never had formal musical training. He organized the Mission San Jose Indians into a well-known 30-piece orchestra. His musicians had uniforms that were purchased from a French ship. Until real musical instruments arrived from Mexico, he made practice instruments. The Indians learned to play and sing complicated songs, many of which were written by the padres. Before coming to the mission, music was an important part of the Indians' lives. They used flutes, drums, and other rhythm instruments to accompany their singing and dancing. At the mission, Indians became skillful at playing guitars, trumpets, flutes, violins, and other European instruments. Rhythm instruments helped them keep the beat. They played many types of music, including religious songs, children's songs, dance tunes, marches, and serenades. People would come from miles around to hear their concerts.

Duran invented a system for teaching Indian choirs to read music. He wrote the notes for the different voices in different colors. All notes in the bass range were black, in the next higher voice red, in the next black with an open center, and in the highest voice red with an open center. Duran only used the key of F flat. The music was handwritten in very large books so that everyone in the choir and orchestra could easily read the notes. The music book covers were wood covered with leather, and the pages were usually made of sheepskin parchment.

Activity

Write a song about life at a California mission.

1. Make up your own tune or use a familiar one.

2. Write words that show what you know of details of life at a mission. For example, your song could tell about the jobs, crops, history, religion, locations, architecture, conflicts, Indians, Spanish, and/or celebrations of the mission(s).

3. Gather friends or family to help you sing the song.

4. You may want to add rhythm instruments to accompany your song.

reproducible

San Francisco de Asis (Mission Dolores)

City: San Francisco
Founded: October 9, 1776
Order of founding: 6th
Founder: Padre Francisco Palou

It took years for the Europeans to find San Francisco Bay due to its narrow entrance and coastal fog. When the Spanish realized the importance of the bay, they decided to build a presidio and two missions there. (The second mission was later built at Santa Clara.)

It was also decided that families should be sent to colonize the area in order to make a stable settlement. A difficult six-month overland journey was taken in 1775–1776 by 240 soldiers, settlers, and their families. The colonists had been recruited from among the poor people of Sonora, Mexico and were offered money, food, and clothing. Juan Bautista de Anza led the colonists and livestock across deserts, mountains, and valleys to Mission San Gabriel and north to Monterey. Several babies were born along the route. They stayed in Monterey while Anza and a small group of men went north to San Francisco Bay. Anza chose sites for the presidio and the San Francisco de Asis mission. The mission was located near a stream that emptied into a small lake surrounded by wildflowers. Anza named the stream Arroyo de los Dolores (Stream of Sorrows), in honor of Our Lady of Sorrows. Even though the lake and stream were filled in long ago, the name Mission Dolores is still commonly used today.

Anza left Lieutenant Jose Joaquin Moraga in charge of bringing colonists to start the presidio and mission in San Francisco. Padre Palou dedicated the new mission on June 29, 1776, just five days before the signing of the Declaration of Independence. On August 18th, the ship *San Carlos*, brought supplies to the presidio and mission. It was the first ship to sail into San Francisco Bay.

On October 9, 1776, when the mission buildings were almost finished, there was a great celebration. There was a parade, fireworks, firing of cannons, chanting, and singing, but the Indians didn't come.

The noise of the celebration frightened the Indians so much that they weren't seen for several days. Then their enemies arrived from San Mateo, attacking and burning one of their villages. The San Francisco Indians scattered again, escaping across the bay in tule rafts. The Indians were only seen occasionally at first, when they came to hunt ducks on the lake. It was almost a year before the first three Indians was baptized.

The mission grew slowly. The land was too sandy for good crops. The cold, foggy weather bothered the Indians. The Indians ran away from the mission to hide among the more carefree tribes across the bay, where it was difficult and dangerous to locate them. Sickness also took the lives of many Indians. The Indians had no immunity against the European diseases that the Spaniards brought. When the Indians got sick, they had trouble getting well in such a damp, cold climate.

In 1783, the foundation of the present church was laid in a location less swampy than the original site. This adobe building was dedicated in 1791. Mission Dolores was built in a strikingly simple style, without the usual arches and arcades. Even though it is probably the least restored of all the missions, it is in remarkably good condition. The original bells still ring on special days.

After Padre Serra's death, Padre Palou left the mission and returned to Mexico to write a book about Serra's life. Padres Martin Landaeta and Antonio Dante came in 1785. Under their leadership, many buildings were completed, but these padres were more strict and not as kind as Padre Palou.

After secularization, the church was used for various purposes. In 1845, the mission lands were sold but were later returned to the Catholic Church by a presidential proclamation. Parts of the mission were leased for private use. For a while, it housed a print shop and the famous Mansion House Tavern.

When the Gold Rush hit in 1849, the sleepy town of San Francisco became a busy city almost overnight. The area around the mission became a center of gambling, horse racing, and drinking. Piece by piece, the quadrangle disappeared, but the church remained in good condition. The mission regained importance as the parish church in booming San Francisco.

The church survived the earthquake of 1906; just a few tiles were shaken off the roof, and some statues and tombstones were damaged. The raging fire that followed the earthquake the next day was stopped in a heroic effort just across the street from the mission! Today, Mission Dolores is the oldest intact building in San Francisco. Masses are still occasionally celebrated there.

In the late 1860s, a larger church was built next to the old mission church. It was dedicated in 1876. It did not withstand the 1906 earthquake. After a delay in construction during World War I, it was rebuilt and dedicated in 1918. In 1952, Pope Pius XII named it a basilica, an honorary church of the Pope. The stained glass windows show the 21 California missions.

Creating Fog in a Bottle

The weather at Mission Dolores was often cold, windy, and unhealthy. The damp, chilling fogs made it difficult for the Indians to recover from European diseases that they caught from the Spaniards. They had no immunity to these diseases and got sick in devastating numbers, often dying.

Fog is created when air is cooled to a temperature below its dew point, forming tiny droplets. A warm, damp breeze is chilled by the cold ground. Tiny droplets of water join together to form small clouds. As the tiny clouds grow larger because of additional droplets, they also become thicker and thicker until the entire area is covered with fog. Fog is just fine particles of water floating in the air near the ground—actually, a stratus cloud at ground level.

Activity

You can make fog by following these steps:

1. Pour very hot water into a clear soda bottle or other transparent container. For safety, do this with the help of an adult. Then pour most of the water out.

2. Quickly put a stiff piece of large-holed screen on the mouth of the bottle. Place several ice cubes on top of the screen.

3. Hold a piece of black construction paper in back of the bottle. Watch the fog form in the bottle.

4. *Here's what's happening:* Warm air holds more moisture than cold air, and warm liquids evaporate faster than cold ones. When the warm air inside the bottle rises and combines with the moist, cool air at the top, fog forms in the bottle.

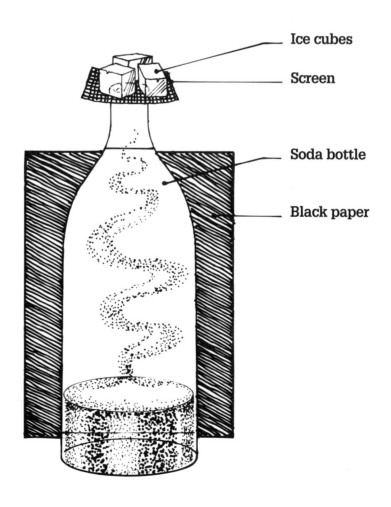

Ice cubes
Screen
Soda bottle
Black paper

San Rafael Arcangel Mission

City: San Rafael
Founded: December 14, 1817
Order of founding: 20th
Founder: Padre Vicente de Sarria

Many Indians got sick and died at Mission Dolores from European diseases that the Spanish introduced. They had no resistance to diseases such as measles, chicken pox, and smallpox. It was difficult to recover in the damp, foggy, cold climate. As an experiment, sick Indians, bundled in blankets, were rowed across San Francisco Bay to the area that would soon become San Rafael. The missionaries hoped that the sick Indians would recover in this warmer, drier climate where the hills offered protection from the chilly ocean winds. After a few weeks, the Indians showed improvement. A hospital was set up as an asistencia, or branch mission, to Mission Dolores. San Rafael was also established to keep the Russian sea otter hunters from moving further south along the coast.

Padre Luis Gil y Toboado from La Purisima Mission volunteered to run the hospital at San Rafael. He was the only padre in California with medical training. On December 13, 1817, the missionaries "planted and blessed with solemn ceremonies the holy cross" at sunset. Padre Gil helped the mission become very successful. Soon, the sick from other missions were also being sent to San Rafael. Gil worked so hard to heal the Indians that his own health suffered. After two years, he was sent to another mission.

Padre Juan Amoros took over and helped the mission become self-sufficient, more than just a hospital. He was very energetic and taught the Indians many trades. Many Miwok Indians came to live at the mission. Amoros asked to have San Rafael Arcangel become a full mission. On October 19, 1822, permission was granted.

Amoros was well-liked by most Indians. He thought of others before himself. For dinner he only ate dried corn roasted over coals, but he carried grapes, raisins, and figs in the sleeves of his robe for the Indian children. Amoros did have difficulty with Marin and Quintin, Indians who turned against the mission. They were imprisoned, but later both worked as sailors. Marin County and the San Quentin prison were named after them.

When Padre Jesus Maria Vasquez Marici del Mercado arrived, life became difficult at the mission. He treated the Indians strictly and often lost his temper. Once, he thought the mission was going to be attacked. He gave the neophytes guns and sent them out to attack the unfriendly Indians before they could attack first. Twenty-one lives were needlessly lost. Del Mercado was removed from his job for six months.

The buildings were quite simple, without elaborate architecture. In addition to the church, there was a long wing for the padres' quarters, workshops, storerooms, and hospital wards. There was no attempt to make it fancy like earlier missions in the south. Its floors were made of dirt, and the windows were only slatted openings; glass was expensive and hard to get. There were a few wooden benches inside. The walls were apparently not decorated. It was one of the few missions where no quadrangle was ever built. Instead of in a bell tower, the bells hung from a wood frame in front of the church.

San Rafael was the first mission to be secularized. General Mariano Vallejo took over the lands and livestock that should have gone to the mission Indians. Vallejo even took grapevines and fruit trees to his private ranches. He felt that the Indians were not able to care for their lands. He "protected" them by gathering the Indians to work on his own ranches. By 1842, most of the Indians had left the mission.

The Mexican governor, Pio Pico, sold the mission, but the sale was invalidated by the Americans. In 1855, the mission was given back to the church by a special presidential decree. The mission buildings were abandoned and a small chapel was built nearby. By 1861, the buildings were sold to James Byers, a carpenter. He demolished the buildings to get the valuable hand-hewn beams. During this time, the orchard and vineyard were sometimes used as a campground by travelers. Nothing remains of the original mission.

In 1869, St. Raphael's church was built as the parish church on the approximate mission site. St. Raphael's burned down in 1919, but rebuilding started later that year.

In 1949, a replica of the mission was built beside St. Raphael's church with a grant from the Hearst Foundation. A star-shaped window was built in the replica, like the one at Mission San Carlos Borromeo in Carmel. This window probably did not exist in the original mission. Sketches of the mission vary greatly. Even the sketch that many historians feel is the most authentic was made from memory by General Vallejo when he was in his 70s.

History of Medicine

Activity

Research the history of medicine.

Rank these medical discoveries in the order in which they occurred. Number the order of events, with number 1 being the oldest. Write the date of each discovery.

Order	Medical Event	Approximate Date
_____	Discovery of X-rays	_____
_____	First scientific study of human anatomy	_____
_____	Trephining head surgery first used	_____
_____	First successful organ transplant (kidney)	_____
_____	First use of ether, the first practical anesthetic	_____
_____	Gene therapy used to treat patients	_____
_____	Proof that diseases have natural causes, not supernatural causes	_____
_____	First vaccine used (against smallpox)	_____
_____	Modern nursing profession started	_____
_____	Learned that certain bacteria cause certain diseases	_____
_____	Discovery of bacteria, which helped lead to the germ theory of disease	_____
_____	Penicillin discovered, the first antibiotic drug	_____
_____	First use of a permanent artificial heart	_____

When the Spaniards came to California, they brought diseases that were common in Europe, such as measles, smallpox, chicken pox, and mumps. Since these diseases were new to Indians, they had no immunity against them. Even if only three to four people caught the disease, hundreds of Indians would soon be sick. The treatments that the Indians used against their own illnesses were not effective against these new diseases. Many thousands of Indians died.

It took many years for modern medical treatments to be developed and to learn what causes disease.

San Francisco Solano Mission

City: Sonoma
Founded: July 4, 1823
Order of founding: 21st
Founder: Padre Jose Altimira

Padre Jose Altimira arrived at Mission Dolores in 1819 from Spain, full of missionary enthusiasm, eager to convert the Indians, and wanting his own mission. He was concerned about the bad weather, Indian epidemics, and poor soil at Mission Dolores. He developed an ambitious plan to close the missions at Dolores and San Rafael. He would combine them into one large mission farther north. Without the knowledge or approval of the Padre Presidente Vicente Sarria, Altimira got approval from Governor Luis Arguello and the Territorial Assembly in Monterey in 1823. Altimira founded the mission at Sonoma in what he called the Valley of the Moon on July 4, 1823. He called this new mission the "New San Francisco de Asis." When the Catholic Church finally found out, they were upset with the governor and Altimira, because only a padre presidente could decide to build a mission. Sarria ordered construction to stop until a compromise was reached. The Sonoma mission was allowed to remain under the name San Francisco Solano, but the other two missions would not be closed. Solano was the only mission founded after Mexico's independence from Spain.

The mission was also considered important because of the threat of the Russians, who had established outposts at Bodega Bay and Fort Ross along the California coast. The Russians had started settlements in Alaska; but in 1812, they sailed down the California coast searching for sea otter furs and agricultural lands. The Spanish government wanted to push the Russians out of the area. They felt that a new mission in Sonoma would help convince the Russians that California belonged to Spain.

Altimira's church was a crude wooden building covered with whitewashed mud. It was dedicated on April 4, 1824. Mission Dolores sent cattle and church supplies. Even the Russians sent gifts to this new mission, such as linens and a bell.

Altimira was not popular among the local Pomo and coastal Miwok Indians. Instead of using kindness and understanding, Altimira ruled with flogging and imprisonment. Many Indians ran away. In 1826, angry Indians revolted against his harsh treatment. After the harvest, they stole crops and burned some of the wooden buildings. Altimira was forced to escape, eventually returning to Spain.

Altimira was replaced by Padre Buenaventura Fortuni, who served the mission from 1826 to 1833. He was much kinder to the Indians, and many returned to the mission. Under his leadership, a large adobe church was built in 1833, and most of the quadrangle was completed. Fortuni then requested a transfer to a mission where there would be another priest to help share the responsibilities. At age 58, he didn't feel able to run the mission by himself.

Shortly after Fortuni left, the Mexican government secularized the mission. General Mariano Guadalupe Vallejo took over as the manager of the mission property in 1835. During the mission years, he had been in charge of the soldiers and town of Sonoma. Vallejo was responsible for building the present chapel in 1840 because of the large church's decay. The roof tiles and timbers had been taken from the church by the people of Sonoma for their homes.

The unprotected adobe walls slowly dissolved. The chapel was built as a parish church on the site of Altimira's original wooden church.

Vallejo took over the mission and divided the land among the Indians as he was required to do. Many Indians gave back the land in return for room, board, and protection. He sold some of the mission lands to his relatives and became wealthy. He owned a 66,000-acre rancho. His job was to keep order in this part of the Mexican territory and to support the soldiers, and he was responsible for colonizing new towns. He took grape plants from the vineyards at San Francisco Solano for his own property.

After the Russians withdrew from Fort Ross in 1841, attention turned to the increasing number of Americans in California. These Americans became concerned that the Mexicans might force them to leave. On June 14, 1846, about 30 to 40 Americans took over Sonoma and made Vallejo a prisoner. They made a homemade flag with a grizzly bear, star, and the words "California Republic." They declared California an independent republic by flying the flag over the Sonoma Plaza. The flag looked similar to today's California state flag. The Bear Flag Republic lasted 23 days. Before any major trouble started, United States troops captured Monterey on July 7th and raised the American flag. Vallejo was released from prison and played a big role in the beginning years of the state of California.

The mission was sold in 1881, because the buildings were too dilapidated to save. Over the years, mission buildings were used as a barn, blacksmith shop, saloon, and winery. In 1903, the Landmarks League bought the ruins, which were turned over to the state of California. Damage from the 1906 earthquake slowed restoration. After several restorations, the mission is now part of the Sonoma State Historic Park.

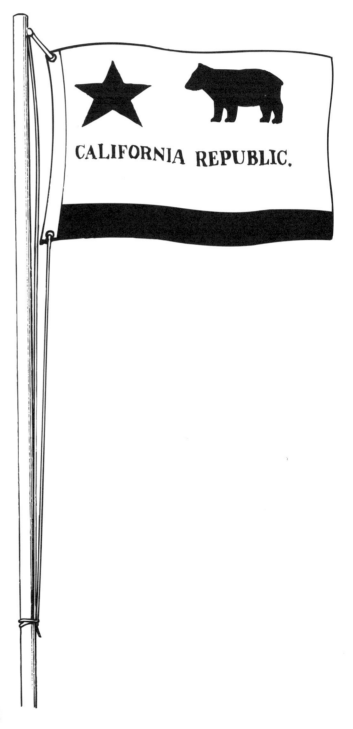

San Francisco Solano Activity

Stained Glass Paintings

In the dining room of the San Francisco Solano Mission is the Virgil Jorgensen memorial collection of California mission paintings. Virgil's father, Chris, traveled by horse and buggy with his wife in 1903–1905 to study the history and architecture of each mission. His 61 paintings show what remained of the missions during those years.

Chris Jorgensen (1859–1935) was born in Norway and came to San Francisco as a boy. He studied at the California School of Fine Arts and later in Italy. He became well known for his oil and watercolor landscape paintings, especially of Yosemite and the missions.

Virgil became interested in the San Francisco Solano Mission after ranching near Sonoma. He served on the mission's advisory board in the 1940s as the mission was being restored. He felt that this mission was a wonderful place to display his father's collection of watercolor paintings of the missions.

Activity

Create a stained glass painting of one of the missions.

San Francisco Solano is known for its collection of mission paintings. You can create one, too. Use the stained glass painting technique described below:

Directions

1. From a firsthand visit, photograph, or sketch in a book, lightly sketch one of the missions with pencil on white paper. Keep the sketch simple, just drawing the basic shapes of the building, windows, and doors.

2. Paint over the pencil lines of the sketch with black paint. Let the paint dry.

3. Paint inside the black lines with the appropriate colors. Let the paint dry.

4. Use a brush or rag to lightly rub cooking oil to the back of the paper. This will increase the transparency of the paper, making it look like stained glass when held up to light.

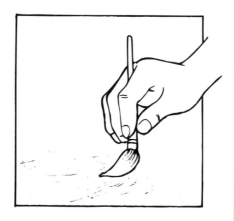

Results of the Mission Period

Some Indians benefited from the missions and others did not. At the time of the founding of the first mission, there were at least 300,000 Indians living in Alta California. They lived in about 105 small nations and spoke at least 100 different languages and dialects. Within the first few years, many of these Indians died from diseases such as measles, since they had no immunity to European diseases.

The Indians who survived helped build the missions. Each Indian had a quota of labor to complete each day or a required number of hours to work. In return, they received Christian sacraments, food, clothing, and education. They agreed to follow Spanish customs and learn about Christianity. During the mission period, nearly 88,000 Indians were baptized. They also learned skills such as caring for livestock, farming, making tallow into candles and soap, blacksmithing, carpentry, tanning hides into leather, manufacturing adobe bricks, weaving and spinning, making wine and olive oil, cooking, and making roof tiles. Missions worked toward self-sufficiency and, although such commerce was illegal during part of the mission period, they conducted trade with passing ships. They grew a wide variety of crops, and ranches supported large herds of livestock.

By becoming Catholic converts, the Indians gave up their freedom. They became known as neophytes (meaning "newly planted") and belonged to the missions. The Indians had to move to the mission compounds or one of the nearby villages. If they tried to escape, they were hunted down and, if captured, brought back and punished. Many Indians fled the missions because they missed their former homes, resented the missionaries' attacks on their former religions and traditions, feared European diseases, hated regular work hours that they were not accustomed to, and disliked punishments. Critics of the mission system say that it was a thinly disguised form of slavery.

Many other Indians, however, enjoyed mission life and were very fond of the padres. They liked the reliable, varied food supply; protection from enemies; and the rich ceremonies of the Catholic Church. The mission system was a peaceful approach to settling new lands for colonial expansion. This was a time in history when conquering soldiers from other countries would not have treated the native cultures as humanely as the padres had.

The people of New Spain wanted to be free of Spain's rule. In 1810, they broke away from Spain, and for over ten years, they fought for their independence. Finally, in 1821, they won their freedom and changed the name of their country to Mexico. The effects on the missions were far-reaching. Supplies and funds rarely arrived. The missions had to support themselves and also supply the pueblos and military.

The new Mexican government passed a secularization law in 1833 (that was carried out over many years) that each mission was to become a parish, or "secular" church, for the people of the nearby pueblo. The land was to be divided three ways. Part was for town pastures and agriculture. Part was for the town itself. Also, each Indian family was to be given land for a home and crops. Secularization had worked well throughout the Spanish empire but was a disaster in California. Governor Figueroa tried to divide the lands equally between the Indians and Mexican citizens, but many government officials weren't honest. The Indians didn't understand the new Mexican laws and were often cheated out of their land.

After the secularization of mission property, the Indians no longer had the mission as the focus of their lives. They had no land, homes, or animals. Usually they didn't have their former tribal organization to return to because so many Indians had died from diseases. They were displaced peoples, often exploited. Some Indians returned to their old ways of life; some became servants of the new owners of mission lands; some died from hunger and illnesses; and some drifted to the pueblos.

Ironically, the padres came with the best of intentions. They saw the Indians as children—lost souls needing the sacraments of God and benefits of European civilization. Each mission was to hold the property and wealth in trust until the Indians were appropriately "civilized" and could form a Spanish pueblo. The intent was that this would happen within ten years. The Indians were not ready to take over in so short a time. Had it been given enough time, secularization might have been successful.

Within a few years, resources of the missions such as land, crops, and livestock had been dispersed. Except for the few chapels that served as parish churches, most of the missions were abandoned and soon turned to ruins. The wooden roof timbers rotted, then collapsed beneath the weight of the heavy tile roofs. With the roofs gone, the adobe walls were exposed to the weather and melted back down to the earth from which they had been made. Over the years, the missions were used in a variety of new ways—as barns, saloons, stores, and barracks.

After the United States declared war against Mexico on May 13, 1846, U.S. naval forces, under command of Commodores John D. Sloat and Robert F. Stockton, attacked the Pacific Coast of California, while a troop of soldiers under Stephen W. Kearny crossed overland. When Mexican forces in California surrendered, a peace treaty was signed at Guadalupe-Hidalgo on February 2, 1848. Under the terms of the treaty, Mexico ceded California to the United States. Just nine days before the treaty was signed, James Marshall discovered gold along the American River in California. News of this gold discovery soon spread around the world. The massive Gold Rush greatly increased the population of California. On September 9, 1850, President Millard Fillmore signed the admission bill, making California the 31st state to enter the Union.

In the 1850s and 1860s, the United States Land Commission reevaluated the legal standing of the ownership of the mission lands and buildings. The U.S. government returned many missions to the church, but by then many were in such poor shape that they could not be used.

Starting in the 1860s, there was new interest in the European influence of the missions. Many new buildings, such as those at Stanford University, founded in 1885, adopted the Spanish colonial architectural style. The first attempts at restoration of the missions often mixed architectural styles; for example New England-style bell steeples were put on top of old mission churches. More recent reconstruction emphasized re-creating the buildings as they appeared in their prime. Architects and historians did research in old journals, looking for sketches that would give clues to mission details. Much of the reconstruction was initiated by the Native Sons of the Golden West, the California Historical Landmarks League, and the Landmarks Club. Today, the mission chain is visited by more people than any other historical sites in California.

EL CAMINO REAL

Answer Key

Nuestra Señora de la Soledad:
Naming the Missions (pages 63–65)

1. San Juan Capistrano
2. San Luis Obispo de Tolosa
3. San Diego de Alcala
4. Santa Clara de Asis
5. La Purisima Concepcion
6. Santa Ines
7. Santa Barbara
8. San Rafael Arcangel
9. San Buenaventura
10. San Fernando Rey de España
11. San Gabriel Arcangel
12. San Juan Bautista
13. San Francisco Solano
14. San Luis Rey de Francia
15. San Miguel Arcangel
16. San Jose
17. San Antonio de Padua
18. Nuestra Señora de la Soledad
19. San Carlos Borromeo del Rio Carmelo
20. Santa Cruz
21. San Francisco de Asis

San Rafael Arcangel:
History of Medicine (page 87)

1. Trephining head surgery first used—8000 B.C.
2. Proof that diseases have natural causes, not supernatural causes—400s B.C.
3. First scientific study of human anatomy—1543
4. Discovery of bacteria, which helped lead to the germ theory of disease—1670s
5. First vaccine used (against smallpox)—1796
6. First use of ether, the first practical anesthetic—1842–1846
7. Modern nursing profession started—mid-1800s
8. Learned that certain bacteria cause certain diseases—mid to late 1800s
9. Discovery of X-rays—1895
10. Penicillin discovered, the first antibiotic drug—1928
11. First successful organ transplant (kidney)—1954
12. First use of a permanent artificial heart—1982
13. Gene therapy used to treat patients—1990

Bibliography

The California Missions: A Complete Pictorial History and Visitor's Guide edited by Elizabeth L. Hogan (Menlo Park, CA: Sunset Publishing Corporation, 1993). Very informative book, including mission history, meaning, maps, recipes, charts, and visitors' guide, plus extensive paintings, photographs, and information on each mission.

California Missions: A Guide to the State's Spanish Heritage by Gregory Lee (Frederick, CO: Renaissance House, 1992). Information on the locations, driving directions, and details of the history and unique features of each mission. Also includes a short history of the mission system, biographical sketch on Padre Serra, and state map. This is a small, yet comprehensive guide that is easy for tourists and students to use.

California Missions Coloring Book by David Rickman (New York, NY: Dover Publications, Inc., 1992). Not only is this a coloring book that children will enjoy and adults find interesting, but the book includes a detailed introduction about mission life and history. Each page includes a detailed picture and lengthy, informative caption. Not just for children.

The Decoration of the California Missions by Norman Neuerburg (Santa Barbara, CA: Bellerophon Books, 1991). Mission decoration history, materials, artists, design sources, locations, motifs, decorative elements, and mission-by-mission details are explained. Extremely detailed drawings and information.

From Fingers to Finger Bowls: A Lively History of Early California Cooking by Helen Walker Linsenmeyer (San Luis Obispo, CA: EZ Nature Books, 1990). California's history, as shown through historical anecdotes, illustrations, recipes, and cooking methods from Indian days to 1900.

The Indians and the California Missions by Linda Lyngheim (Chatsworth, CA: Langtry Publications, 1990). Each mission is described, including a drawing, history, daily life, and information about the mission today. There are also details of Indian life and Spanish explorations.

Live Again Our Mission Past by George Kuska and Barbara Linse (San Mateo, CA: Arts' Publications, 1992). Helpful book for teachers and students, including information on California Indians, Spanish explorers, mission history and ways of life, activities, and details of each mission.

Mission: The History and Architecture of the Missions of North America by Roger Kennedy (Boston, MA: Houghton Mifflin Company, 1993). Includes details of the religions associated with the missions, cultural details, and mission architecture; contains spectacular photographs.

The Missions: California's Heritage by Mary Null Boule (Vashon, WA: Merryant Publishing, 1988). Series of 21 booklets for students, one on each mission. Each booklet starts with the same introduction to the general history and way of life at the missions. The last half of each booklet concentrates on a specific mission, the mission today, and mission history. Boule has also written a series of 26 booklets for students called *California Native American Tribes*.

Missions of California by Don J. Baxter (San Francisco, CA: Pacific Gas and Electric Company, 1970). Details of the overall history of the missions, plus the way of life and history of each mission.

The Natural World of the California Indians by Robert F. Heizer and Albert B. Elsasser (Berkeley, CA: University of California Press, 1980). Comprehensive book detailing the tribes, languages, territories, lifestyles, and history of the California Indians.

A Sense of Mission: Historic Churches of the Southwest by Thomas A. Drain (San Francisco, CA: Chronicle Books, 1994). Twenty-nine of the most beautiful and historically important churches in Texas, New Mexico, Colorado, Arizona, and Southern California are described and photographed. Also included are architectural details, information on cultural diversity and religious significance, and visitor information.

Tales and Treasures of California's Missions by Randall A. Reinstedt (Carmel, CA: Ghost Town Publications, 1992). Fascinating stories and legends of seven California missions, including tales of pirates, lost treasure, bandits, and shipwrecks. High-interest material for children.

Whispers along the Mission Trail by Gail Faber and Michelle Lasana (Alamo, CA: Magpie Publications, 1986). Complete book for children covering the exploration of early California, the founding and description of each mission, daily life at the missions, pueblo settlements, and mission restoration.